D-DAY
SURVIVOR

D-DAY SURVIVOR

SURVIVOR

AN AUTOBIOGRAPHY

HAROLD BAUMGARTEN

PELICAN PUBLISHING COMPANY
GRETNA 2015

Second printing, April 2015

Library of Congress Cataloging-in-Publication Data

Baumgarten, Harold.
  D-Day survivor : an autobiography / Harold Baumgarten.
    p. cm.
  Includes bibliographical references and index.
  ISBN-13: 978-1-58980-421-0 (alk. paper)
  1. Baumgarten, Harold. 2. World War, 1939-1945—Campaigns—
France—Normandy—Personal narratives, American. 3. United States.
Army. Infantry Regiment, 116th. 4. World War, 1939-1945—Regimental
histories—United States. 5. Soldiers—United States—Biography. I.
Title.
  D756.5.N6B384 2006
  940.54'21421092—dc22
  [B]

                                                   2006025313

Printed in the United States of America

Published by Pelican Publishing Company, Inc.
1000 Burmaster Street, Gretna, Louisiana 70053

To my devoted wife Rita, who has been subjected to my frequent, painful flashbacks and periodic surgeries for more than fifty-five years. She encouraged me to go to medical school, write my books, and speak about D-Day.

To my wonderful children, Karen, Bonnie, and Hal, whom I am very proud of and love.

To my grandchildren Michael, Rose, Samantha, Katy, Matthew, and Rachel, who are very precious to me.

To my surviving Army buddies, who prodded me to write down my D-Day memoirs.

Lastly, to my buddies who lost their lives on D-Day, but will forever live in my heart and prayers.

Contents

Preface

In 1994 and 1999, the first and second editions of *Eyewitness on Omaha Beach* were written. Those editions were released to coincide with the fiftieth and fifty-fifth anniversaries of D-Day. After many sold-out printings and reprintings, I was going to retire from book writing. However, a small voice inside me kept saying, "Once you are gone, the true story of D-Day will be lost." Thus, I decided to write a third, more complete, and autobiographical book.

Over five years, I have amassed, with the help of friends, a tremendous amount of information about D-Day. This information must be shared. God saved me on D-Day to be the spokesman for those true heroes who perished on the sand and bloody-red, swirling waters of Dog Green Sector of Omaha Beach. They must never be forgotten.

D-DAY
SURVIVOR

I

Growing Up

THE EARLY YEARS

When one speaks about their life, the best way to start is with birth. I was born in Lebanon Hospital in New York City in 1925. My folks were thrilled that I was a boy. My brother, William, had died at age seven months from scarlet fever. Two sisters were already in the family, Ethel, age 8, and Beatrice, age 5. Being the youngest child, and a boy, was very advantageous. I was a "spoiled child," a state especially fostered by my mother.

As far as family, it was my sweet four-foot, nine-inch, bluish-gray-eyed, raven-haired mother who taught me to read and write at age three. She was an excellent cook and baker. Mom Rose was the eldest of sixteen siblings. Until she met and married my Austrian father she worked for Macy's Department Store in New York City. Rose had to commute from the family farm in Colchester, Connecticut, to work at Macy's. Weekdays, she boarded with an aunt in New York, and she returned home for weekends. That aunt happened to be my father's sister-in-law. My father, Morris, immigrated to the United States from Austria as a teenager and taught himself to read and speak English. He was my first hero, a self-made man. Morris was very skilled in metal-work and construction from the old country. His patriotism for the United States was extreme, but when he tried to enlist in the army during World War I, he was rejected as an enemy alien. My sisters Ethel and Beatrice were of another generation.

I also enjoyed visiting my maternal grandparents in Easton, Pennsylvania. My grandfather, Martin Weitzman, had his own horse. My grandmother, Rachael, had a large talking parrot. These were fun distractions. My mother's family was so large that I had a multitude of cousins. When we had a family reunion, it had to be held in a large amuse-ment park in town.

I was brought up in Harlem in an Irish-Catholic-dominated neighborhood. My first best friend was an Italian boy, Joey, two years my senior. Joey's mother, from Italy, wanted to feed me all the time. At that time, I really didn't appreciate the good Italian food. Even though I was Jewish and attended a synagogue, I learned about and respected my neighbors' religious beliefs. I was able to go to their churches, funerals, and wakes. My elementary school, P.S. #125, was integrated, so I developed no racial prejudices. In fact, I felt very much at home there, especially since all the teachers had already taught my two sisters. All this helped to shape my social beliefs for later life.

Though open to others' ways of life, I am unwavering in my own religion. I remember, when I was about four years old, seeing a movie about Jewish martyrs in ancient times. Romans and Spaniards burned them at the stake. As they were dying, they prayed the *Shema,* a Hebrew prayer specify-ing the belief in one God. This vivid memory has had a tremendous influence on my beliefs in religion. My belief in God has always been steadfast. I pray every day. The thrust

Hal Baumgarten, age 9, in Easton, Pennsylvania.

of my prayers has always been for good health for my family, my friends, and myself.

A smart, docile child, I was very good in school, in both behavior and learning. My mother helped me with my homework and studying. Having a photographic memory gave me the ability to assimilate schoolwork with ease. I excelled in spelling and math in elementary school.

A large city like New York is a cultural banquet, with all its museums, excellent libraries, and showplaces. There was no shortage of things to do or of friends my own age. The streets outside our apartment houses, with its parked autos, became our daily playground. In warm weather we played "stick-ball," and the street became a baseball diamond. In the winter, when the streets were covered with snow and ice, it became a one-man sledding downhill and snowball-fight paradise. My friend Joey and I played on our scooters on the campus of Columbia University. We also played around Grant's Tomb, which was in our neighborhood. On President Grant's birthday, his and his wife's mausoleum was opened for viewing.

Playing on the tough streets of New York City toughened me up. I was once hit over the head in a fight with an iron roller skate, requiring sutures from Sydenham Hospital Emergency Room. On another occasion, while climbing a steel fence in Morningside Park, I impaled my left wrist on one of the spikes. Once again I became a visitor to the ER. My father made the hospital a large copper kettle in appreciation. It is interesting to remember that the hospitals in those days reeked with the smell of ether.

About age nine, my family and I moved to the borough of the Bronx. I now lived in a Jewish neighborhood. The schools were more modern and the curriculum was much richer. I enjoyed the physical training and music appreciation courses. My athletic life began in the Bronx. I was a small child compared to my peers in elementary and junior high school. However, I worked hard to build my body and become muscular. I played baseball, football, track, tennis, boxing, and even hockey. I belonged to an athletic club at the 92nd Street YMHA, to which I traveled every weekend by subway to compete. Though at fourteen I was five feet, seven inches tall and weighed only 125 pounds, I worked out in basketball and track with the USA Club and memorably won a silver medal in a 1939 decathlon against high-school seniors. The medals I won during this period are still in my possession.

I was given Hebrew School training between ages eleven and thirteen. At one time, I could read and write Hebrew like a native. At age thirteen, I was bar mitzvahed. With my unbelievable memory, I was able to read from the holy Torah and make a three-page English speech without notes. Around the time of my bar mitzvah, I was also honored to be the best man at my sister Beatrice's wedding.

Advancing in my studies, I attended Macomb's Junior High School, which was a terrific school to attend. I departed for school early, in order to play handball before classes. The curriculum was great and varied. We studied French, American history, and advanced math as well as woodworking and electric wiring. Here too I excelled in sports. As an eighth grader, I hit a three-hundred-foot home run over a thirty-foot-high wall, a play that allowed my class team to win the school's softball championship. The gymnasium was kept open in the evenings for community use. I played basketball there with a team called the Admirals.

Away from school I found any way I could to continue my athletic games. In the street fronting our apartment house, I was able to play a New York City game called "stick-ball." It was played like baseball, except the bat was a broomstick, broom removed. The ball was a rubber one by the

Hal Baumgarten's bar mitzvah, March 1938.

Spaulding Company. In the winter, when the street was covered with snow and ice, we sleighed downhill. We used a one-man sled with a steering mechanism. Touch football was another of our big street games. There was never a dull moment, but none of my friends, nor I, indulged in drugs or alcohol.

After graduating from Macomb's, I attended the prestigious Bronx High School of Science. It was a great school, walking distance from my home. However, after only one year I transferred out in favor of a school with an athletic program, DeWitt Clinton High School. This school, located in a park, looked like a college building, built of light bricks, three stories high, with a tower in the middle. The student body was all male. When I attended, the school had 12,600 students. We had three shifts for our school hours; I attended from 8:00 A.M. until noon. Sounds bad, doesn't it? However, when I started college, I realized how well prepared I was. The biology, physics, trigonometry, and French courses gave me a great educational foundation. Besides track and baseball, I went out for the soccer team. In retrospect, playing soccer in the U.S. in the 1940s was revolutionary, as soccer has only become popular in our country in recent years.

While in high school, weighing 165 pounds, I was playing football for money. I played under the name of Harold Babe, since at that time money from any sport would make you ineligible for all college athletics. I earned as much as twenty-five dollars per game kicking field goals for a semi-professional football team. In the 1940s, this sum was considered big money, especially for a sixteen year old. Incidentally, I never thought of kicking a football like a soccer player. In those days, people would have laughed at that. Though I found great satisfaction in the pursuit of sports, my parents were not attuned to athletics, and I had to sneak out of my house to play on Sundays. The equipment I used had to be stored in another player's house. My father only watched me play on one occasion; that day I kicked a forty-three-yard field goal. He wasn't impressed. During that season I received one bad injury playing, a sprained or fractured ankle; however, I played the rest of the season with the ankle taped.

My entire life did not revolve around sports, however. My social life was great. We had neighborhood parties and dances. We danced to the big bands like Tommy and Jimmy Dorsey, Glenn Miller, Harry James, and Benny Goodman, who frequented Broadway in New York City. People like Frank Sinatra sang at the Paramount Theater. We didn't have television in our time, but I was introduced to it when I attended the 1939 World's Fair, where they demonstrated that new technology. Instead of TV, my friends and I were entertained by *The Lone Ranger, Green Hornet,* and *The Shadow,* radio programs. We also had a popular music program called the *Hit Parade,* which played the ten top songs for each week.

Another exciting activity of my youth was travel, which my folks enjoyed. In 1936 and 1937, I went on cruises with them on the Swedish-American liner *Gripsholm.* We visited Havana, Cuba; Kingston, Jamaica; Port-au-Prince, Haiti; and Nassau, Bahamas. These were interesting places for a young person to see, and the weather was delightful. There was great poverty in all of these places, except Havana, Cuba. On this island nation, people were very friendly and the Cuban food and music were great. The Cuban economy was flourishing, even though the country's citizens were under a dictator, Fulgencio Batista. As a mark of the island's prosperity, Havana boasted a huge capitol building, almost a copy of that of the United States. Under its dome was a glass case in the floor. I was amazed to discover that this round glass case held a twenty-five-carat diamond.

In 1939, we went on a long driving tour that has left me with vivid memories. Traveling north from New York City, we arrived at the St. Lawrence River. At that time the river was unpolluted and cmerald green in color. There were islands in the river, known as the Thousand Islands, and I saw Irving Berlin's island home, whcre he likely wrote "God Bless America." I was able to swim in the St. Lawrence and Lake Ontario. We then drove to Niagara Falls, which we viewed from both the U.S. and Canadian sides. There I happened to meet a girl friend from home, with her parents; however, she soon caught the mumps and had to return home. As we visited Canada, I noticed that the motion picture *The Wizard of Oz* was playing. Exploring farther into Canada, my family visited a beautiful botanical garden at Hamilton, Ontario. Then we visited Montreal, where I was able to practice my junior-high-school French. We also viewed a magnificent church on a very high hill, called the Sacred Heart of Saint Andrew. From there, we returned home, traveling through beautiful New York State. Our stop at Fort Ticonderoga, of Revolutionary War fame, gave us a great view of Lake Champlain. Saratoga was interesting, with its special spring drinking water and horse racing. It was summer time and the New York State grapes and cherries were delicious.

Though our trip to Canada had been one of pleasant sights and beautiful locations, the harsher reality of the war that had erupted in Europe surfaced during our vacation. While the United States was in isolation, Canada was involved with England in World War II. As a result, I saw Canadian soldiers guarding strategic facilities. Within two years, America would be joining World War II, but only after suffering a disastrous attack.

The attack on Pearl Harbor occurred while I was still in high school. My classmates and I were all anxious to enter the service, but I was too young. On Pearl Harbor Day, I was playing in a football game in George Washington High School's stadium. I was buoyed up by returning a fifty-yard kick, but was dragged down by the sadness of this day's momentous event.

In February 1942, at age sixteen, I was accepted to the very prestigious University Heights Branch of New York University. Though this campus no longer operates as part of NYU, University Heights was at that time a small branch of the largest privately endowed college in the United States. It was a wonderful school that offered in its country atmosphere a stadium, track, tennis courts, Hall of Fame of Great Americans, and a compulsory ROTC program. The ROTC there had its own building and rifle range and scheduled a full-dress parade every Thursday, reviewed by a U.S. Army general. I was in the school's infantry battalion, and thus I was in an army uniform by 1942.

At the age of seventeen, I tried to enlist in the Army Air Corps. My parents lived in Florida a good part of the winter, and I had to have my sister sign so that I could enlist as a minor. I wanted to be a navigator, as I was fascinated by their ability to guide a plane so exactly. However, I was turned down for flying duty because of exophoria of my left eye (lazy eye syndrome). I refused ground duty. Therefore, I remained in the ROTC Infantry at New York University. We used the U.S. Army General Manual, paraded, and qualified firing weapons on our rifle range.

As far as my social life, we had campus dances and parties at Lawrence House, a social hall. I had many girlfriends, but at that time, I had the "old fashioned" belief that sex was only for married people. In fact, if I had died in World War II, I would have departed as a virgin. My first sexual experience was on my twenty-first birthday. One of my girlfriends was determined to give me a good birthday present.

After a year at the school, I had been transferred to the Arts and Science college, where I majored in science and history. Though the school canceled its football team during the war years, we did have an active intramural program, and we played touch football on the campus. Being on the baseball and track teams balanced my educational and athletic experience. The best way to make a college sports team was to obtain an athletic scholarship. Without one, an athlete was considered a "walk-on" in a general tryout. Even as a walk-on I made the baseball team; however, I had to wear a uniform that said "freshman." In college athletics in the 1940s, freshmen were not allowed to play on the varsity teams. One day in the spring of 1943, a talent scout named Barrett offered me a Yankee Stadium tryout. He had observed me hitting balls about four hundred feet in batting practice. I was not a great catcher, but I could hit the long ball. In my tryout, I batted against a left-hander, Mario Russo. I put three balls into the left field stands. Barrett planned to use me for the Newark team of the American Association. But before I could begin playing for the team, I was drafted into the U.S. Army.

With two years of college and ROTC, I received my draft notice at age eighteen on June 26, 1943. I was happy to receive the notice; it was time to enter the service and repay our country for all the benefits extended to my family. Applying for a college exemption was not on my agenda, even though my professors were on my draft board. On July 10, 1943, I entered the U.S. Army.

II

The U.S. Army

BASIC TRAINING

On July 10, 1943, I was on my way by train to Camp Upton, Long Island, New York. This is where Irving Berlin composed "Oh How I Hate to Get Up in the Morning." We were given many inoculations and issued helmets, uniforms, and shoes. There were written tests given to us. I must have scored very high on the Army Aptitude Test, because two officers made remarks about my grade. "This is your ticket to go to Officer Candidate School," they said.

On July 13 we were on our way by train to Camp Croft, South Carolina. Here I had my first experience with eating ham. On the chow line, I was served boiled cabbage and a red meat. I surmised it was corned beef and cabbage. To the soldier next to me I said, "This corned beef is good." He replied, "You are eating ham, not corned beef."

At Camp Croft, I was housed in a large two-story barrack building. Due to my ROTC training, I was made an honorary corporal, though I would remain, in fact, a private throughout the war. I wore a black armband with two stripes on it. In our parades, I was at the front of our platoon as "guide on."

We were issued our own M-1 Garand rifles, each with its own serial number, which we had to memorize. We learned how to take the rifles apart and put them back together, blindfolded. Each soldier's rifle had to be cleaned and oiled and kept in "A-1" condition. In combat, it would be our best friend.

Sergeant Dreisen was in charge of our platoon. He was a strict disciplinarian, but very fair. His aim was that we be trained to be good soldiers, and he advised us that our learning now would save our lives later. I did become a good soldier. On the rifle range, I was almost perfect at every distance. Being a good athlete, I completed all the twenty-mile marches, infiltration courses, and hand-to-hand combat fighting courses with ease. I also took part in athletic events. I practiced, especially on weekends, with the camp's baseball team.

While I was at Camp Croft, my father flew down to visit me one weekend. This experience was terrific for him, as he had never been in an airplane before that time. We had a steak dinner and beer at the Cleveland Hotel in Spartanburg.

At the end of our training, we went on what was called "bivouac." During this time we camped out and practiced maneuvers in the woods of South Carolina. On our way to the bivouac area, our column was repeatedly attacked by radio-controlled miniature airplanes. When under attack, we would run off the road and take cover from the bags of white powder the planes released. If hit with the powder, you were considered a casualty. When we arrived in the bivouac area, we put up pup tents, which house two people. Each soldier carried half of his tent and tent poles. On our maneuvers in the forest, we were trained to look out for mines and tree snipers. Our trainers would place these obstacles in our paths. For the first time in my life, I caught poison oak and suffered blisters and sores on my hands and arms. The itching was unbearable, but at least I didn't have to serve on KP, or kitchen police, where soldiers had to peel potatoes and clean pots and pans.

After my seventeen weeks of basic training, I was kept in camp while the rest were shipped out. I was to undergo Army Specialized Training at Clemson College. I heard that Mel Allen, a notable radio sports announcer from New York City, was in the Thirty-sixth Battalion, also stationed at Camp Croft. At New York University, the baseball coach had assigned me to call in our game scores to Mel Allen to broadcast on his evening program. Mel, in later years, became the "Voice of the New York Yankees" and was the broadcaster for all of their games. I decided to visit him, and when I arrived at his barracks, he had just marched in from the rifle range. He was dirty and full of sweat. I asked him how he had come to be assigned to the infantry, to which he responded, "Someone goofed up on my records." About two weeks later, he was transferred to a special services outfit.

During my time in Camp Croft, we received weekend passes to go into the town of Spartanburg. Even though it looked like a small town, it was the third largest city in South Carolina and home to Wofford College. Unfortunately the army often gave us injections for diseases like yellow fever or typhoid on Friday afternoons, ruining the weekend with headaches and fever. When we did get to enjoy our weekends, many of us relished a steak dinner and beer for about $1.50 at the Elite restaurant. There were also USOs in town and two hotels. I enjoyed playing ping-pong at the First Baptist Church in town. One weekend I received a pass from the base chaplain to travel to Asheville, North Carolina. To go farther than Hendersonville, which was fifty miles away, I had needed a special pass. In Asheville, we had a party and dance with local girls. Their parents, very patriotic people, put us up at their homes and gave us a super breakfast.

Having completed my seventeen weeks of basic infantry training at Camp Croft, I was waiting in camp to begin the Army Specialized Training Program, which I had signed up for in lieu of Officer Candidate School. After waiting two or three weeks for that college program to begin, all the potential candidates were told that the army had canceled the program. We were given two weeks' leave for home and were told to then report to Fort Meade, Maryland. After about one month of advanced infantry training in extremely cold weather at Fort Meade, I was transferred to Camp Shanks, Orangeburg, New York. There we were entertained one evening by a USO show, the Ted Housing Group. Ted Housing was famous for singing and dancing to "Me and My Shadow." At Camp Shanks, I was also able to play basketball. While jumping under the basket for a rebound, I came down and twisted my ankle. It swelled up like a balloon, and I was sent to the base hospital for x-rays. My x-ray was negative, but I could hardly walk. The soldier at the reception desk was a friend from my neighborhood, Arthur Feldman. Even though he was able to go home regularly, he was not satisfied with his desk job. He wanted action and had put in for a transfer. His transfer later came through, and he ended up in the Eighty-third Infantry Division in Europe.

From Camp Shanks I was scheduled to go overseas with hundreds of others, all from the canceled Army Specialized Training Program. Before shipping out, I was able to go home for New Year's Eve. Then I and the other soldiers traveled by train and ferry to a large New York pier on the Hudson River. With my swollen, painful ankle, I limped up the gangplank carrying my heavy pack. Our last names were called, and we answered with our first names and the last four numbers of our Army Serial Number. We were to set sail on the *Ile De France,* third largest troopship in the world. This ship could outrun any German submarine. Thus, the fifteen thousand soldiers and Air Corp men were headed for Europe. We rolled up and down with the rough waves of the North Atlantic and the zigzagging maneuvers of the ship. I became terribly seasick. What a miserable feeling!

We finally docked in Greenock, Scotland, and marched off the ship through an arch, a sign on which read, "Through this arch march the greatest soldiers in the world." It was a morale builder. Red Cross Volunteers fed us doughnuts and coffee as we boarded trains for England. (British trains are excellent.) Looking out the curtained windows, we were able to see the gorgeous countryside of Scotland. We were taken to an army base in Yoevil, England, a replacement depot. While they were deciding where to send us, some of the soldiers came down with the measles, and we were quarantined. Waiting out our quarantine, some of us played touch football; however, our containment lasted ten days.

I was immune to measles, as I had had both regular measles and German measles in childhood; thus, I decided to explore England. I slipped through a loose wire fence around the camp and walked down a country road. Ultimately, I came to a pub, which in England are family and friend gathering places where they talk, drink, and play darts. I met some very friendly Brits. There were children in that southwest area who had been evacuated from London for safety. I gave the kids our U.S. chocolate and chewing gum. One of the thirteen-year-old boys thought I would be interested in dating his seventeen-year-old sister. He asked, "Are you going to knock up my sister?" In British slang he was asking me simply if I meant to call on his sister. There are several language barriers the American soldiers had to overcome in Britain. For example, a truck is known as a lorry and gasoline is referred to as petrol. We also had to learn about their money. In those days, a shilling was equivalent to twenty cents, a florin forty cents, a half-crown fifty cents, and a pound four dollars and three cents.

I fell in love with the British people because I realized how much they had suffered from bombings and shortages since 1939. They also had lost loved ones in the fighting at Dunkirk and in North Africa. Many had lost friends and relatives from the German strafing and bombing of their cities. Their cities had been leveled and their homes demolished. Though we Americans considered ourselves relatively immune from such destruction, in fact, even our camps in England were bombed occasionally.

Three weeks after arriving, a select group of replacements from the U.S. were sent to Crown Heights, Plymouth, England, where the 116th Infantry of the Twenty-ninth Division was headquartered. Col. Charles D. W. Canham addressed our group from a stage in an auditorium. This man, with the nickname of "Hatchet Face," appeared to me to have the head of a skeleton wearing eyeglasses, but he was every inch a true West Pointer. He told us that we would be the leaders in the second front invasion of Europe and direly predicted that two out of three of us would never return home. In a drawl, he stated, "Anyone who has butterflyze in the bellah, speak up now."

I was transferred along with John Barnes and Russell Pickett to Company A, First Battalion, of the 116th Infantry Regiment, Twenty-ninth Division, at Ivy Bridge, England. Our first evening there, the soldiers who had been stationed there since October 1942 questioned, "Why are they sending kids like you over here?" We were isolated at one end of the camp, in a field, for about one month. The large tent we were billeted in had a dirt floor that became muddy when it rained. There were no heaters, and we were freezing. With me in the tent were Stanley Gembala (from New York), Richard Brantonies (from Oil City, Pennsylvania), Herman Dunham, Jr. (from Virginia), and Irwin Bogart (from Silver Spring, Maryland). In retrospect, out of the fifty of us in that tent, only four of us were going to return to the United States alive.

III

The Stonewall Brigade

THE REAL TRAINING

I was now a member of the famous 116th Infantry, "The Stonewall Brigade." This group has roots in the Revolutionary War. It was a Confederate outfit in the Civil War, under the command of Gen. Thomas Jonathan "Stonewall" Jackson (the regiment's namesake). We were trained for one month by Sgt. Clyde Powers of Bedford, Virginia, until we were considered "good enough to join the regulars." After this probationary period, we were housed in Nissen huts, with a small potbelly stove in the middle for heat. Thank God! My sleeping bunk was a bag full of straw supported above another buddy's bed by metal straps. We were always armed, so my loaded rifle hung from the wood of the bed. In the adjacent bunk was Pfc. John Powers, Clyde Powers' brother. He was one of the best soldiers with whom I had the good fortune to serve. A former member of the disbanded Twenty-ninth Rangers, he was handsome, rugged, and very knowledgeable. I learned much about soldiering from this great guy. He was one of the "Boys from Bedford" killed in action on D-Day.

During the training of the 116th, we marched at a record-setting pace across the British countryside, twenty miles at a time with full, heavy field equipment. This training would enable us to hit our enemy fast and hard. There is a similarity here to the troop training given by General Jackson during the Civil War. Our training at Ivy Bridge and on the moors above our camp included hand-to-hand combat, throwing hand grenades, making explosive charges, firing our weapons, and qualifying for the Expert Infantry Badge. It was a lonely time for me; I missed my parents and home. I wrote home to my folks almost every day.

In March, I received my first weekend pass. Pfc. Hal Weber, a Company A scout, and I went to Torquay via train. It was my nineteenth birthday, March 2, 1944. Our photo was taken by a street photographer, and we attended the cinema. Afterward we had orange milk and crumpets. Before we knew it, we had only five minutes to make the last train for Ivy Bridge. We ran all the way to the station, only to find a closed fifteen-foot iron gate. In our superb physical condition, we scaled the gate and made the train back to camp in time.

Later in March, we were transferred by train to Wales, near the cities of Braunton and Woolacombe. Here we lived in tents and worked everyday to prepare for the invasion. We practiced fitting into mock-up wooden landing craft placed on the Woolacombe sands at the Amphibious Training Center (ATC). At a signal from our officer, our boat team would run out of the make-believe assault boat and fan out to the right and left so that the BAR (Browning Automatic Rifle) men were positioned on each flank. The riflemen and two bazooka men were in the middle, along with the men carrying the explosives, wire cutters and Bangalore torpedoes, and flamethrowers. This disembarkment exercise was repeated over and over until it became automatic.

Another part of our training involved our personal

Hal Baumgarten in Torquay, England, on his nineteenth birthday, March 1944.

Hal Baumgarten and Hal Weber in Torquay, England, on Baumgarten's nineteenth birthday, March 1944.

weapons. For example, one of our instructors had us slide feetfirst into a beach crater with a BAR. While lying on our backs, with our feet against the gun's bipod and the butt held against our chins, we had to fire the weapons. The Air Corps was to provide us with these craters in an actual battle, and the rationale was that we would be less exposed when firing in that position. We also practiced firing our bazookas at the openings of cement pillboxes. Two men were assigned to this rocket gun. The assistant gunner was supposed to release a clip that held the shell and then tap the gunner on the shoulder to let him know it was safe to fire. During one of our exercises one of the assistant gunners failed to release the clip, and the rocket sent the gunner and his weapon careening into a sand dune. He was lucky not to have been blown up.

Perhaps the most challenging exercise was ascending a rope-ladder cargo net on the mock-up of the side of a ship. Loaded with our weapons and about eighty pounds of equipment, we had to climb the net to the top. It was like scaling the side of a five-story building. The first day, on reaching the top platform, I asked the instructor when I was going to climb down the net. I was told to go down the metal pipe superstructure to the rear. Some of these pipes were more than six feet apart, and with the metal nails on the soles of my shoes, I thought I was going to fall and be splattered all over the Woolacombe sands.

As a finale to our training, we made some landings from our mock assault boats, using live ammunition to attack pillboxes. Before each of our landings, the area was saturated with 80 mm mortar shells. On one occasion, the bombardment was not lifted in time, and Acey Peacock was wounded in his upper lip. With the lip severely scarred, he returned to the outfit in time for the invasion. He was killed in action on D-Day. We used Bangalore torpedoes, five-foot sections of metal pipe, filled with explosives, to blow aprons of barbed wire. The pipes were made to be screwed together into as many sections as needed to reach the target, and they were set off by a blasting cap, fuse, and fuse-lighter at its rear. The beauty of the Bangalores was that they would blow up the barbed wire aprons sideways, not toward the soldiers in the front. It enabled us to blow a path through many rows of barbed wire rapidly.

The more realistic landings on Woolacombe Beach used actual LCAs (Landing Craft Assault boats) of the British navy with live ammunition, artillery shells, and tanks. Landing dry, we attacked pillboxes on the beach with bazookas, flamethrowers, and satchel charges (a box of TNT attached to a two-by-two pole of wood with a hinge and set off by primer cord, blasting cap, fuse, and fuse-lighter). To assemble the satchel charges, we connected twenty to forty pounds of TNT to a primer cord, which looked like an innocent yellow and black cord, though it was itself a powerful explosive. A strand of primer cord, wrapped around a tree and set off, could cut the tree in half. The hinge on the pole served to keep the enemy from pushing the satchel away from the pillbox's aperture.

We also went on two complete landings on Slapton Sands Beach in southwest England. These were Operations Fox 1 and Fox 2. The latter was the final rehearsal for the invasion, at the end of April 1944. Each time we boarded the same ship as we would for the real invasion, the HMS *Empire Javelin*. At Slapton Sands, which had the same topography as Normandy, we again attacked pillboxes on the beach. There we saw the dual-drive amphibious Sherman tanks for the first time. These tanks, our secret weapons, were able to swim in to the beach like assault boats, drop their rubberized canvas boatlike sides, and quickly target their 75 mm cannons directly at the pillboxes. After our attack on the

Company A, 116th men in Camp D-1, left to right, Lt. Ray Nance, Lt. Edward Gearing, Lt. John Clements, and 1st Sgt. John L. Wilkes.

beach defenses with our weapons, we proceeded up the bluff to attack empty homes above the beach. These gorgeous homes had been evacuated by patriotic Brits at Christmastime. In every one of these operations there were losses of lives and casualties, which were hushed up.

In between our rehearsal landings at Slapton Sands, there was Operation Tiger. This was an ill-fated exercise by the U.S. Fourth Infantry Division during which German E-boats sunk transports and LSTs (Landing Ship Tanks). Seven hundred fifty U.S. servicemen lost their lives, but the disaster was kept secret for decades.

Our next move was to a huge camp at Blandford, England, in early May 1944. Here we lived in tents, and new equipment was issued. The old equipment was destroyed in bonfires, and some of the old ammo exploded in the fires by accident. This camp had a mammoth sand-covered field in a valley-like area, and we took advantage of the space as a parade ground. We had a full-dress Twenty-ninth Division parade led by the division's band. Our helmets and bayonets were polished with oil to make them shine in the sunlight, and we were reviewed by the high-ranking officers of the Supreme Allied Command. This was my first and last parade with the Twenty-ninth Division. Many of the soldiers who took part in this event were dead within the month.

In preparation for the invasion deployment, we packed our barracks bags full of coats, sweaters, underwear, toilet articles, and personal effects. These bags were stenciled with the first letter of each soldier's last name and the last four digits of his army serial number. They were supposed to meet us in France at a future date. I gave away my dress shoes and hat to one of our Black army truck drivers. Many of us, including myself, had our heads shaved so that our hair could not be grabbed during hand-to-hand combat.

Around May 15, we were transported by truck to secret camp D-1, about ten miles north of Dorchester, England. These camps were called "sausages" because of their shape. Our camp was surrounded by barbed wire and armed British soldiers. Nobody was allowed in or out without written orders. The camp's tents were filled with the entire First Battalion, 116th Infantry, their company headquarters tents, a large kitchen tent, and a tented movie theater. My Company A was tented in the northeast corner of the camp. We dug foxholes in the calcified English soil to protect ourselves from air raids. For our physiological needs, there were outhouses with collecting pails. The Brits collected the pails and burned the excretions for fertilizer. The acrid odor of the smoke was very unpleasant. On the campgrounds, in the southwest corner, was a large British manor house. It was from the steps of this grandiose building that

Maj. Gen. Clarence Huebenor, commander of the First Infantry Division, addressed us. We were advised, not to our satisfaction, that we would be under his command for the first twenty-four hours of combat. Along with the Sixteenth Infantry of the First Division, the 116th would attack the western (most heavily defended) part of Omaha Beach in the first-wave assault.

IV

Omaha Beach Defenses

THE KILLING FIELD

Omaha Beach was the code name for one of the two U.S. beaches on the northern Normandy coast. It was four and a half miles long by three hundred yards wide at low tide. Utah beach, located to the west, was the other U.S. beach. They were both part of the German Atlantic Wall, which extended from Norway down to Spain. When military commanders get together to plan for a victorious battle, they seek three elements: high ground, superior firepower, and manpower. The German High Command had it all on Omaha Beach, especially at the Dog Green sector.

Gen. Erwin Rommel took command of the German defenses in January 1944. His strategy was to stop any invasion in the water and on the beaches. Not one enemy soldier must get off the beaches alive. Thus, he put his men to work building four rows of diabolical obstacles on all the beaches, starting with the first one, 300 yards out. From there rows of obstacles were spaced at 50-yard intervals toward the land. The obstacles at 300 yards out were called element C or Belgium gates and were cemented into the beach. Seven feet wide by 10 feet high, these were constructed of heavy iron to block assault boats. In row two, closer to land, the poles were placed. The poles, wooden or cement, were cemented into the beach and topped with Teller mines, sometimes referred to as "asparagus." Row three contained the ramps, each composed of a log supported by two bipods of wood elevating the log to a forty-five degree angle, pointing toward land. These ramps were placed so that the assault boats would crash into them, throwing men out the rear. At row four, about 120 yards from the beginning of the beach, the Germans placed hedgehogs (the most common obstacle seen in D-Day photos). These were three steel rails welded together and cemented into the beach. They stood five feet high. There were other obstacles designed to stop tanks, but those mentioned were the important ones for the invading soldiers. The obstacles were all barbed wired and mined, and only visible at low tide. Since low tide at Normandy in June 1944 was at 0630 hours, the invasion had to take place at that time so that the soldiers could see the obstacles and try to avoid them.

The First Battalion of the 116th Infantry, my outfit, was assigned to invade the Dog Green Sector of Omaha Beach. This sector was located on the right, or west flank, of Omaha, the smallest, but most heavily defended part of that beach. Dog Green was only nine hundred yards long by three hundred yards wide during low tide, which made it too narrow to land entire battalions abreast of each other. This sector was the part of Omaha Beach portrayed in the two motion pictures *The Longest Day* and *Saving Private Ryan*. A twenty-five-foot cement seawall extended the entire length of the beach. It tailed away from the beach at a forty-five-degree angle and was covered with loose shale stones. The top of this wall was covered with barbed wire and mines. Looming over the wall was a one-hundred-foot bluff covered by the greenery of summer. Thirty feet above the seawall, zigzag trenches connected to a cocoon of underground tunnels were cut into the bluff. These trenches had three machine guns and many riflemen, some with telescope sights. There were cement emplacements, called Tobruks, on the bluff, from which they fired their 105 mm mortars at the beach. At the top of the wall, built into the bluff, were three huge pillboxes, which the German's numbered WN 71, 72, and 73. The sides of the pillboxes facing the beach were covered by greenery of the bluff. At the top of the bluff, three miles south of the village of Vierville-sur-Mer, was the German artillery. They were dug in cement emplacements, with each of their 88 mm canons pre-targeted on every square foot of the beach below. In fact, all the German weapons had been zeroed in on the beach. To make their artillery even more accurate, they had forward observers in the steeple of the Vierville church and in the zigzag trenches on the face of the bluff.

A six-hundred-yard road on the left side of the beach meandered from left to right uphill into Vierville-sur-Mer. This road was of great strategic value to the Allied command. How else would the invaders get their equipment, tanks, trucks, artillery, and jeeps into France? It was code named D-1, or Dog-1. Two of the pillboxes on the left could defend this road: one fired a 75 mm cannon eastward, and the other had a 50 mm gun on a swivel, enabling it to fire both east and west. The road also had a machine gun emplacement at its right, or west entrance, from the beach.

In the motion picture *Saving Private Ryan*, Tom Hanks' character is shown shouting and trying to communicate,

"Dog 1 is not open." D-1 was not open for a good reason. The Germans had built two 8½-foot-high parallel walls, 6 feet thick, blocking the entrance of D-1 from the beach. In front of the walls were a tank trap, barbed wire, and mines. In *The Longest Day,* Robert Mitchum, playing Brig. Gen. Norman D. Cota, Twenty-ninth Division, spent the last scenes of the movie trying to blow these walls. This attempt was falsely portrayed. The infantry was not stopped by these walls. When these walls were finally blown, at about 5:00 P.M. on D-Day by Col. Robert Ploger of the Twenty-ninth Division Engineers, General Cota was already in Vierville. He captured the town with the aid of Company C, 116th Infantrymen, and some of Company C, Second Battalion Rangers.

A third huge pillbox was located all the way on the extreme right flank at Pointe de la Raz Percé, camouflaged as a seaside cottage. This fortification, known as WN 73, could fire its machine gun, an MG42, sideways down the entire length of Dog Green sector. So the Germans had the high ground and great firepower. What about the German manpower on Dog Green sector? They were believed to have 250 elderly, poorly equipped and disciplined men of the 716th Wehrmacht Division (static troops), made up of conscripts from Poland and White Russia. The information on troop numbers was supplied by the French underground, or Marke, who were in the practice of informing Eisenhower's headquarters by means of two carrier pigeons carrying identical messages. If one got lost the other might still get through. These brave Frenchmen transmitted that these soldiers "would surrender rapidly." Unfortunately, in May 1944 both pigeons sending updated information on German manpower were shot down by a German soldier with a shotgun. Thus, Allied headquarters were not privy to the information that the Germans had moved in 200 young, well-trained men of the 352nd Grenadier Division into the area. These men were part of Germany's best soldiers in Normandy. They now had 450 men defending the bluffs at Dog Green sector.

The *Empire Javelin* was anchored off the coast of Dog Green beach at 3:30 A.M. on June 6, 1944, D-Day. This ship held the men of Companies A, B, C, and D, First Battalion, 116th Infantry Division, who were picked to invade this fortress at Vierville. They were part of the "Stonewall Brigade." Later William Geroux, reporter for the *Richmond Times-Dispatch,* aptly called them the "Suicide Wave."

V

The *Javelin*

OUR MOTHER SHIP

On March 17, the paymaster of Company A issued us two one-hundred-franc notes. This was invasion money, worth four dollars U.S. In the headquarters tent of Company A, there was a clay model of the Dog Green sector of Omaha Beach. Also, they had aerial photos of the German soldiers working on the beach obstacles. Thus, we knew where we were going, what we were facing, and it was frightening. I wrote home to my sister Ethel, asking her to get the government telegram before my folks obtained it. My mind was made up that I was not going to live through the invasion.

On May 23, we were saddened by a tragic accident. Sixteen members of Boat Team #1 of Company B, 116th Infantry, were involved in an accidental explosion of a dud shell on a rifle range. Four of them were seriously wounded or killed. Clifton O. Palmeteer, Jr. (Kent Store, Virginia) was badly wounded in his legs and was subsequently returned to the States. From Company A, Pvt. Robert Palmer and I were transferred to Company B, along with fellows from other outfits, to replace the injured in Boat Team #1. One of the

French invasion money issued to Company A, 116th Infantry soldiers, May 1944.

fellows was Pvt. Robert Dittmar (Fairfield, Connecticut). Thus, I was now in Company B. I remember seeing the bloody uniforms and smashed equipment lying in front of the Company B headquarters tent as I relocated.

The company clerk, Sgt. Robert Bleeker (New Jersey), took me to the tent of my new boat team of "strangers." Sergeant Bleeker also gave me a special pass to go into Dorchester for a Friday evening religious service on June 2. I found out in later years that he, too, was Jewish. He admonished me to keep quiet and not show my French currency during my trip into the city.

Now a part of Company B, I formed a close friendship with Pfc. Robert Garbett, Jr. Bob was a twenty-five-year-old Company B regular from the Newport News, Virginia, area. He was a tough soldier, though a gentle-looking five-foot, eight-inch-tall, blond-haired and blue-eyed man. We discussed our lives, future hopes, and dreams. His wife in Oxford, England, was pregnant. It was interesting to read each other's mail out loud. He took me under his wing and helped me in any way he could. He made me a watchband from his leather garrison belt because my watch was irritating my wrist. It was Bob who convinced me not to wear the issued combat jacket. He said, "Hal, don't wear it, because it will drown you." Instead, as an act of defiance, I drew a large Star of David on the back of my field jacket with "the Bronx, New York" printed around it. The reason I took his advice was that he was an "old man" of twenty-five, and I was a "kid" of nineteen.

My new boat team members who watched me drawing on my jacket with my Eversharp ink pen thought I was crazy. They warned, "If you get captured, they will cut your nuts off." I knew the Nazis were persecuting Jews. They were making these defenseless people wear Stars of David on their clothing. I wanted the Germans to know who I was.

On June 3, we took all our equipment and marched to the southwest corner of Camp D-1. The Twenty-ninth Division trucks were waiting to transport us south to Weymouth. We disembarked at Weymouth and started marching in formation along a boardwalk. On my right was a very high bluff, which had hotels, apartment houses, and businesses. To my left was a magnificent harbor where hundreds of warships, transport ships, and mine sweepers were docked. This was part of the great D-Day armada. The local people lined the side of the boardwalk, flashing the "V for victory" sign and wishing us good luck.

We came to a pier and were ferried out to our familiar "mother ship," the *Empire Javelin,* by means of LCA assault boats. We boarded the ship by climbing up cargo nets, which was difficult due to our heavy equipment. Our entrance from the main deck was through a blackout curtain and then down about ten steel steps that led to a huge, gray-painted room. On the right side of the room were canvas cots stacked three high for Company B. On the left side of the room were the same accommodations for Company A. There was no mingling with the British crew, except during mealtime, and later while in the assault boats. I took a lower bunk and piled my equipment and rifle off to the side.

It rained that evening and into Sunday. However, on Monday, June 5, the weather cleared, and I went up on the main deck. I noticed a tremendous amount of activity going on between the U.S. destroyers and cruisers, with their blinking Morse code lights. In the harbor most of the ships had barrage balloons floating above them to ward off enemy air attacks. I noted a decoy wooden radio-controlled ship.

About 3:00 P.M., Chaplain George R. Barber held a religious service on the deck for us. Attendance was voluntary, but the main deck was crowded. He advised us to pray to God in our own way to guide and protect us in the morning. I said my *Shema* Hebrew prayer. At 5:00 P.M. our ship started to sail out of the harbor. I went forward to the bow to have a better view. There, standing next to me was a Twenty-niner who was short, bald (except for some red hair around his ears), obese, and about forty-five years old. What was he doing in a Twenty-ninth Division uniform? Our guys were rugged looking, with an average age of twenty-four. He introduced himself to me as Morris Saxstein of New York. His outfit was Headquarters, Company A, 116th Infantry. This unlikely member of our young fighting force apparently had a vendetta against the Nazis. I had the feeling, from his accent, that he was probably a German Jewish refugee from Hitler's persecution. He said, while puffing on his pipe, "All I want is one German, but you, Hal, will be a hero in the morning, whether you like it or not."

I never saw Morris again, except in what I think is his photo on page 41 of Joseph Ewings' *History of the Twenty-ninth*

Division in World War II and in some other books and documentaries. In this famous photo, he is being rescued from his sunken assault boat. U.S. Army records list him as being lightly wounded in action June 6-9, 1944. I have a lot of respect and admiration for this interesting stranger.

I didn't eat much that evening because the food on the ship was terrible. My main food was a few Cadbury chocolate bars. After eating I found the shower room, a large room, painted gray, with six showerheads. I took a cold seawater shower there about nine o'clock. I had to use a bar of lava soap, which felt like sandpaper. After a change of underwear, I put on my old #10 football jersey. Then I put on my wool, gas-impregnated uniform. I had a headache, because it was stuffy in the large wardroom. Many of the guys were playing cards or shooting dice. Going over to my buddies in Company A, I found Pvt. Tom Mullins (Worster, Massachusetts), an aidman. He gave me two APCs, equivalent to two adult aspirins. Who knew, in those days, that aspirin would cause you to bleed more profusely on being wounded? By this time I had made my peace with God and was convinced that I was not going to survive; however, I wanted to be brave in the morning for myself and my buddies. At 10:00 P.M., I took the "secret" maroon seasick capsules, later known as Dramamine. At 11:00 P.M., we heard General Eisenhower's stirring message to us over the PA system. We now realized for certain that this was the real McCoy. He said:

> Soldiers, sailors, and air men of the Allied Expeditionary Force! You are about to embark upon the Great Crusade, toward which we have striven these many months. The hopes and prayers of liberty-loving people everywhere march with you. In company with our brave allies and brothers in arms on other fronts, you will bring about the destruction of the German war machine, the elimination of Nazi tyranny over the oppressed peoples of Europe, and security for ourselves in a free world.

VI

The Trip to the Beach

ALONG WITH STRANGERS

We prepared to get dressed for combat. My steel helmet, adorned with its blue and gray Twenty-ninth Division monad insignia, was covered with camouflage netting. Carried in the right side of the netting was a blasting cap crimped to a fuse and fuse lighter. This was to be used, in conjunction with a half-pound of TNT in my left rear trouser pocket, to aid in blowing a foxhole. A double-tubed life preserver extended from beneath each armpit to clip under my chin. The CO_2 capsules used to inflate the life preserver were adjacent to its clip. The preserver in turn covered a small black rubber bag containing a gas mask specially designed for D-Day, with the canister built into the mask. Along with its large viewing windows, it allowed great mobility. My fellow soldiers put on their special invasion combat jackets, which I chose not to wear. These jackets were made of a dark-green canvas material with built-in packs (four in the front and two in its back). Metal grommets encircled the waist of each jacket and these were used for hanging hand grenades. I put on a regular army pack connected to a harness, which clipped on to it. This would enable me to discard the pack rapidly, if necessary.

My pack contained, along with the usual army things, a change of underwear, socks, a mess kit, and three days' supply of D-rations. Along with my specially lubricated thirty-caliber M-1 Garand rifle, I carried three hand grenades, bandoleers with black-tipped armor-piercing ammo, clips of BAR ammo, a pick shovel, a razor-sharp pocketknife, and a ten-inch bayonet stone sharpened on each side. The lubricant for the rifle was invented by scientists in order to keep the French sand from fowling its moving parts. I carried a special first-aid kit strapped around my right thigh. Besides a bandage and sulfur powder, it contained (for the first time in U.S. Army history) a Syrette with one grain of injectable morphine sulfate. This Syrette, reminiscent of a miniature toothpaste tube, had its own built-in hypodermic injection needle. We wore gas-preventative-impregnated wool olive drab uniforms, canvas leggings, and blucher-type hobnailed shoes (also gas impregnated). My wallet was in my left shirt pocket, containing family photos and the two one-hundred-franc bills. We were also issued, along with the seasickness pills, three barf bags. They gave us plioform bags to protect our weapons from the sea; however, I covered the tip of my rifle with a rubber condom. All this clothing, equipment, and armament weighed well in excess of one hundred pounds.

The men of the First Battalion of the 116th were young, the best-equipped (up to that time), well trained, disciplined, and very patriotic soldiers. Their average age was twenty-four. Standing an average of five feet, seven inches tall, and weighing on average 147 pounds, some of these men had to carry their own weight in equipment.

Our landings were going to be made in LCAs, the British version of the U.S. LCVP (Landing Craft, Vehicle, Personnel) or Higgins boat. They were a little longer, but smaller inside, than their American counterparts. Their sides were lower than the Higgins boat, and they sailed lower in the water due to some thin armor plating, which made them more prone to take on water. Of course, there were no seats or head coverings for us; thus, the men carrying all this heavy equipment would have to stand up for three hours in a very crowded space.

The training landings at Slapton Sands were a picnic compared to D-Day. The practice landings were done in daylight, in calm seas. We had climbed down the cargo nets into the boats and were usually landed in dry conditions on the beach. The pillboxes we attacked were on the beach itself. On D-Day, the weather was so bad that we would have to be lowered over the side of the *Javelin* into our LCAs by davits.

We loaded up our gear and at 3:15 A.M. went up to the main deck. I shouted good luck to my Company A buddies as I struggled over the railing to get into our LCA. There were twenty-nine men and one officer to each boat as well as three young British sailors. Each man knew his position in the boat. I was the fifth man on the left side of the boat, behind Clarius Riggs of Pennsylvania. He carried a BAR, for which I carried six twenty-round metal clips in my cartridge belt. There was a lot of shouting and chatter, until our boat hit the water. Then suddenly there was silence, and the mood of the men became very somber. I assume many, including myself, were thinking of home and family, and praying.

The towering gray-black waves smashed against our small boat, attempting to swallow it up. All the boats were tossed around like matchsticks. We were all immediately soaked by the icy English Channel's ten- to fifteen-foot waves. The bilge pumps were not capable of handling all the water in the boat, so we had to bail out the water with our helmets.

There was not only water in the boat, but also floating vomit. Unlike so many others, I was not afflicted by the vomiting caused by seasickness. My theory for not vomiting was to chew gum, suck on candy, and keep swallowing. Intent, I watched the orange-red glow of fires visible on the horizon. These fires were about ten miles away and were the result of the Allied bombing of France. The Allies were trying to destroy bridges, rail lines, and communications. They were aided by the sabotaging activities of the heroic fighting French underground. All this dealt much confusion to the Germans.

While we prepared our approach of the French shore-line, Hitler, the evening before, had taken his usual sleeping pill and didn't awaken till about 2:00 P.M. Gen. Erwin Rommel said, "No idiot would attack in this weather." He returned to Germany for his wife's June 6 birthday. The present he brought her was a pair of French shoes.

There was no way to anticipate the horrors of the holocaust that awaited us on the Dog Green sector at Vierville-sur-Mer; however, we knew that the beach had been prepared over a four-year period. It was considered an impregnable Atlantic wall. General Rommel had ordered his troops to halt, in the water, any invasion on the beaches. But at 3:30 A.M., twenty-four LCAs (six boats to each company), or 720 First Battalion combat soldiers, were on their way to attack 450 defenders on our sector. It would be three hours of standing and freezing in the water until we landed. I was nineteen years old, five-foot, ten-inch, 180-pound, Hal Baumgarten, fifth man on the left side of Boat Team #1 of Company B.

We had the superior manpower. How about our firepower? Each boat was an army unto itself, with riflemen, two automatic weapons, two 60 mm mortars, bazookas, wire cutters with Bangalores, demolition men, and a flamethrower.

We also had the battleship *Texas,* which was to shell Dog Green sector with its huge guns from 5:55 A.M. until 6:25 A.M. (a half-hour). Keep in mind that in the Pacific landings by Marines in World War II, the navy shelled the beaches for two to three days. This sort of barrage would not be effective in France, because the Germans could move up fifty-five divisions to repulse a known landing. In addition the U.S. Navy would support us with an LCI (Landing Craft, Infantry) barge outfitted with one thousand rocket launchers. Right before the landing, they were going to fire four thousand five-inch rockets at Dog Green sector. Navy combat engineers also planned to blow two clear paths through the beach obstacles for the invading soldiers. We even had sixteen dual-drive Sherman tanks assigned to our Dog Green sector. They were going to swim in like assault boats from six thousand yards out (like at Slapton Sands) and roll onto the beach just before our first assault boats landed. Then they would lower their canvas rubberized sides, and the Germans would be faced with sixteen 75 mm cannons and machine guns at point-blank range. Our trip across the beach would be covered by their gunfire.

Unfortunately, the battleship *Texas* had to fire its big guns from twelve miles out, in heavy seas, and their shells went over the beach. Their five-inch rockets landed harmlessly in the water, because their range was off due to the rough seas. Thus, the U.S. Navy's support that morning was ineffective. Even the navy demolition men were only partially successful, because many were wounded or killed. Fourteen of the DD Sherman tanks drowned in the rough seas, and only two reached the Dog Green beach before the invaders. One of these tanks was immediately put out of action by the German artillery. Therefore, we only had the support of one tank when we landed.

Our support from the air too began to unravel. The Army

Air Corps had planned to drop twelve thousand tons of bombs, from about four hundred planes, on Omaha Beach. The bombing was to occur right before the landings. In fact, the troops were promised "man-made" foxholes. But the cloud cover was so bad, the bombardiers had to delay their drop for three seconds. They feared hitting the incoming troops. This resulted in their bombs landing seven miles south of the beach, and killing some Norman cows. The support of the first wave on the Dog Green sector on D-Day was negligible.

It was now 6:00 A.M. on my Rima wrist watch, a present from my father, and it was daylight. The battleship, far behind us on our port side, had begun its firing. We could see other landing crafts floundering and capsizing. Three of Company A's boats had sunk. Only one of the boat team's men was rescued. These men were from Boat Team #5, with Lt. Edward Gearing, Sgt. Roy Stevens (Bedford, Virginia), John Barnes (Holland Patten, New York), and Russell Pickett (Soddy-Daisy, Tennessee). Only their radioman drowned. Two of the Company B boat teams got lost; one landed way to the east and the other to the west. Company D got lost and landed two hundred yards to the east. Company C got very lost and landed miles to the east, in First Division territory.

Due to the short length of our sector—the shortest of any sector assigned on Omaha Beach—we had to land in sequence, but there were only three boats of Company A and four boats from Company B left to land on Dog Green sector. This meant that only 210 men were going to land in the first wave on our beach, against 450 Germans in their fortifications. This gave the enemy a much smaller target of men to zero in on with their devastating firepower.

In my boat, Bob Garbett looked back at me with a smile and made an "OK" sign with his right hand. He was the

Signal Corps Radio (SCR) man in our boat team and was up front with 1st Lt. Harold Donaldson. Bob wore the same equipment as I, except he carried twenty-five feet of primer cord on his backpack. First Lieutenant Donaldson was a six-foot-tall handsome Texan with a thin, black moustache. The sky was black with U.S. bombers, and we yelled up at them to "give them hell." Near them was Sgt. Clarence "Pilgrim" Roberson, a man only slightly known to me. I looked over to my right and exchanged a smile with Pvt. Robert Dittmar (Fairfield, Connecticut). The fourth man on the right side of our LCA, Dittmar was a six-foot-tall, quiet nineteen year old with sandy hair, blue eyes, and large buckteeth. Bob was an intelligent young man who had graduated from a military school. He was usually very serious and didn't make friends easily. In front of me was six-foot, two-inch Pfc. Clarius Riggs. He was very quiet on the voyage to the beach, and anxious to get into action.

It was 6:15 A.M. on my watch, and we heard the frightening sights and sounds of thousands of five-inch rockets headed toward the beach. It is too bad that they did no damage to the fortifications and obstacles, or injury to the awaiting defenders. The white steeple of the Vierville-sur-Mer church could now be seen to our left, on the top of the bluff. This was our guide for finding Dog Green. I could still see the obstacles, with their mines attached, on the beach. Looking down at my watch, it was 6:30 A.M., and some of my buddies from Company A were directly in front of us. They were getting ready to land on the shores of immortality, and I was landing with, except for those few men whom I knew around me, a boat full of strangers.

VII

The Landing

WHEN WILL I DIE?

Our little boat reached Dog Green sector at 6:40 A.M. As we scraped sand, the Company B boat to our left blew up, and we were showered with wood, metal, and body parts. And of course, blood. Our British crew were very young and frightened. They saw the obstacles with their mines, and I couldn't blame them for their fear. They lowered our front ramp, nervously wanting to get back to the *Javelin*. The lowering of the ramp was like a signal for every German machine gun to open up on the exit from our boat. Lieutenant Donaldson and some of the guys around him were gunned down in our LCA. Clarius Riggs was shot dead on the ramp and fell face-down into the water. I dove in behind him, and only my helmet was creased by a bullet. There I was, standing in neck-deep, bloody red water, with my rifle above my head. Remember, I was five feet, ten inches tall on D-Day. What happened to our five-foot, four-inch soldiers? They went straight down in the water when they left the ramp, and drowned. Their heavy combat jackets, weapons, and ammunition were too much for the life preservers to support. As some of them struggled to free themselves from their gear, they were shot in the water. The water was splattered with bullets as we ran through it. It was surreal.

About twenty yards to my left front were two of the surviving DD tanks, with their rubberized sides down. The other fourteen had drowned in the rough seas, with their men in them. Six Twenty-niners were clinging to the one DD tank farthest to my left, and seven were clutching behind the other remaining one. The farther tank had a dead soldier hanging from its turret, which had been knocked out of action. The tank closest to me was firing its 75 mm cannon at the enemy. Thus, there were thirteen Company A men taking cover behind the tanks. I made a very rapid decision not to join them. After all, I was part of a minority. I didn't want any of the guys to ever say, "Look at that yellow Jew."

As we ran across the beach, we saw the twenty-five-foot-high seawall, with its barbed-wire-covered top, and the one-hundred-foot bluff, covered by the greenery of summer. It loomed up from the seawall. We were taking machine gun fire from the trench on the face of the bluff and from a seaside cottage on the right flank. That seaside cottage was, in reality, a camouflaged pillbox built into Pointe de la Raz Percé. The sound of the German machine guns was frightening due to their speed of fire. We were now running on dry sand with our rifles across our chests (at port arms). While running, we witnessed horrible sights, which would become horrible memories for a nineteen year old to harbor. There were men with guts hanging out of their wounds, and body parts lying along our path. A machine gun spray crossed in front of us, from right to left. I heard a loud thud on my right front and felt my rifle vibrate in my hands. It had a clean hole through its receiver, which is in front of the trigger guard. The seven bullets in my rifle's magazine had saved my life. Another instantaneous thud sounded behind me to the left, and that soldier was gone.

Bedford Hoback, Company A, 116th Infantry, was killed in action on D-Day.

I hit the sand behind one of the hedgehog obstacles, whose steel rails didn't afford much cover. To my right Pvt. Robert Dittmar had been hit in the chest. He tripped over a hedgehog, turned completely around, and fell on his back. He was yelling, "I'm hit, ma. Mother," and then he was silent. Horrible! Six feet to my right lay a gravely wounded Nicholas Kafkalas (Pennsylvania). I knew Nick from Company A. About thirty yards to my left front were Bedford Hoback and Sgt. Elmere Wright, both of Company A (Bedford, Virginia). Sergeant Wright, who had had a future as a pitcher with the St. Louis Browns of the American League, was already dead. Bedford was wounded. On my left was Sgt. Clarence "Pilgrim" Roberson, from my boat team. He staggered by me in the now three inches of water. Pilgrim was helmetless, with a gaping hole in his left forehead. His blond hair was streaked with blood. I yelled for him to get down, but the noise on the beach was horrendous. I am certain he couldn't hear me. Reeling to my left, he knelt down facing the seawall and started praying with his rosary beads. The machine gun in the trench on the bluff literally cut him in half. With tears in my eyes, I drew a bead on the shine coming from a German helmet on the bluff. A miracle! My rifle fired, but failed to eject the spent cartridge shell. However, the machine gun fire from that area was silent after my shot. My being an expert rifleman paid off.

I needed my rifle, so I got up on my left knee and tried to force the bolt back with my right foot. This I did, with all the bullets spraying around me. My rifle split into two pieces because the wood had been splintered on each side of the magazine. I saw the smashed seven bullets as I threw away the two sections of my M-1. Nicholas Kafkalas, with his last breath, crawled over to me to return the two pieces. I considered this final act for years afterward. Ultimately, I realized

Pvt. Robert Dittmar, Company B, 116th Infantry, died heroically on June 6, 1944.

that since everything was so one sided, he wanted me to continue fighting.

Now I was weaponless, surrounded by dead buddies, and the pillbox on the right was shooting up the sand around me. I rarely curse, but I lifted my head and swore at the pillbox on the right flank. At that moment, an 88 mm shell went off in front of me. A fragment of it hit me in my left cheek. It felt like being hit with a baseball bat, but the results were much worse. My left cheek was ripped away, the left upper jaw was gone, and teeth and gums were lying on my tongue. My left cheek was actually flapping over my ear as my blood poured out into the now four inches of dirty channel water. The tide was coming in rapidly, about one inch per minute. I washed my face in this water and luckily did not lose consciousness. Gazing in front of me, I saw that Bedford Hoback had been hit in the face with another fragment of the same shell. He died immediately. I thought to myself, *When will I die?*

VIII

Getting off the Beach

I WANTED REVENGE

I knew I had to get off the beach; however, receiving such a destructive facial wound made me feel like my life was over. I had no knowledge of plastic surgery. I decided to get off the beach as rapidly as possible. My equipment was jettisoned by disconnecting a few clips, but my first-aid kit stayed with me, tied around my right thigh. I had difficulty removing my life preserver because the CO_2 capsules accidentally inflated the twin tubes, and my arms were momentarily lifted skyward. Then with the machine guns splattering up the sand all around me, I crawled speedily toward the seawall. At first, I did a "dead man's float" in the incoming tide. The fear of being hit by a bullet at any moment was on my mind.

When I reached the seawall, I noticed that it was flat and parallel to the beach for about two feet then rose up and away from me at a forty-five-degree angle to the beach. It was covered by loose shale stones. Standing at the wall, incredibly unscathed, was Pfc. Dominic Surro of Company A. He was a well-built Georgia friend, about six feet tall and two hundred pounds. Looking at my face with horror and anguish, he pushed me down on the flat part of the wall. He shouted. "Stay here! I am going to get some help." Surro started to run along the wall to the left (east) toward the Vierville Draw, or D-1. I realized instantly that I couldn't remain there because I was still in the line of fire from the machine gun on the right flank. Seizing a rifle from one of my dead Company B buddies, I ran behind Surro. As I ran with my rifle in my right hand, I attempted with my left hand to pull on the hands reaching up to me. These were all wounded fellow "Stonewallers." There was a sudden *clunk* from in front of me. Surro had been shot dead through his helmet by a sniper. *Oh God! Why not me?*

I reached a corner where the wall angled inward (south). This afforded me safety from the pillbox on the right flank, but not the snipers, nor the exploding mortar shells. When I reached the area adjacent to D-1, the seawall towered twenty-five feet above me (where the National Guard Monument stands today). At the base of the wall, lying face down in the shallow, bloody red water, was Robert Garbett, Jr. My best buddy. His head was facing the water at a forty-degree angle to the wall. He apparently had been shot off the wall or spun around by a sniper's bullet. How did this five-foot, eight-inch soldier get out of our boat in water that was neck deep for my height? He had reached D-1 before me, without discarding any of his equipment. His rifle was clutched in his left hand, and around his left shoulder was slung his walkie-talkie radio. His primer cord, bandoleers of ammo, and hand grenades were on his dead body. I started to cry, and my tears ran down red from my bloody face. This was one of the saddest moments in my life.

Climbing up on the wall, I wanted to charge over to the road above; however, calm, cool Pvt. Gilbert Pittenger (Company A, New Ringgold, Pennsylvania) tackled me. At that moment, a hail of bullets came across the top of the wall. He calmed me down, and saved my life. I found out later that Gilbert, too, had already been wounded. On the wall, besides Gilbert, were Donald Szymczak (Pennsylvania) and Fred Kaufman (New York), both on my left. To my right was a fatally wounded Pfc. Harold "Hal" Weber, who died within minutes from an injury to his face. All the Germans had to do to wipe us out was send a squad of armed men down to the beach; however, they felt secure in their huge bunkers, and they were too frightened to leave them. Of course, we would have fought till death.

As reinforcements to the dwindling Companies A and B, Company D, 116th Infantry, was supposed to land within the next fifteen minutes with their heavy weapons. As I previously mentioned, they became lost and landed two hundred yards east of our beach. Their landing was not as catastrophic as ours, but they had some fierce opposition. Capt. Walter O. Schilling, the commanding officer of their company, was killed in the water. Some of their men were also killed as they exited their LCAs. Sgt. Jimmy Hamlin (Jacksonville, Florida) was wounded in his lower extremity. At the seawall, awaiting his evacuation, he prayed from Hebrews in the New Testament. Cpl. Jack Sims (Roanoke, Virginia) was killed. Sgt. John Robert Slaughter (Roanoke, Virginia) was six feet, five inches tall, so he made a great target for the Germans. Though he survived, he was lucky not to succumb to one of the many bullets that riddled his pack with holes. When he reached the bluff, he was seasick, weak, and tired from his ordeal; however, being a great soldier, he cleaned his rifle. Slaughter heard the firing and explosions coming from the Dog Green sector.

Company C was supposed to follow Company D's landing on Dog Green, but they landed way to the east, in the First Division sector. They landed at about 7:30 A.M. and were able to fight completely intact. Ray Scheurer (Kenilworth, New Jersey) was their only casualty. Ray was wounded in the ankle while ascending the bluff.

Two platoons of Company C, Second Infantry Ranger Battalion, were attached to our 116th Infantry Regiment. The Rangers landed on our right flank, on Charlie Beach, not as the motion picture *Saving Private Ryan* depicted, which showed them landing on Dog Green. As they landed, one of their two LCAs was hit by a few German 105 mm mortar shells. They appeared to lose 50 percent of their men almost immediately. However, led by Captain Goranson and Lt. Sidney Salomon, they were able to knock out pillbox WN 73, on the right flank.

We missed these reinforcements at Dog Green. In fact, Gen. Omar Bradley, commander of the First Army, was on the cruiser *Augusta* when he found out about Dog Green and the slaughter that was taking place there. He ordered an immediate halt to all landings on that beach, depriving us of all second- and third-wave support for our fight. Lt. Alvin Ungerleider (Company L, 115th Infantry), from Burke, Virginia, and his men in the second wave were ordered to land to our east. When landing in their large LCI, they were able to cross the beach with no casualties. Donald Van Roosen (175th Infantry), from Pinehurst, North Carolina, landed with the third wave on June 7, also without opposition. We were left on Dog Green to fight and/or die.

IX

The Beach

WHY NOT QUIT FIGHTING?

The beach around 7:30 A.M. appeared as if painted red. The channel water on the beach was red with blood. The dead and wounded floated like driftwood. It looked like the refuse of a wrecked ship instead of bodies and armament. These were once the well-trained, proud men of the Stonewall Brigade. It was an eerie and heartbreaking sight.

We had been trained to attack pillboxes on the beach itself, not elevated ones. None of the firepower that was promised to us was provided. This lack of aid was mainly due to the horrible weather. The aim of the *Texas* and the rocket-firing LCIs as well as the loss of fourteen of our amphibious tanks could all be blamed on the rough seas. The softening up of the beach defenses and the promised "man-made" foxholes by the Army Air Corps were forfeited due to the bad cloud cover. We weren't even provided with smoke grenades as we were at Slapton Sands.

Would it have helped to have attacked at night, as General Cota had argued? Probably not, because the weather still would have fouled things up. Should we have landed in

Alligators (armored floating vehicles with tracks), as General Corlett, of Pacific fame, had insisted? I think not. The poor weather and the accurate German artillery would have been just as devastating. All this "Monday morning quarterbacking" is a waste of time. In retrospect, our mission turned out to be a suicidal debacle.

Capt. Taylor N. Fellers (Bedford, Virginia), commanding officer of Company A, 116th Infantry, had a sore throat and high fever the night before the landing but was not going to allow his men to land without him. At about 0630 hours, he was gunned down in his landing craft. My old Company A boat team, #6, with 2d Lt. John Hussy, Staff Sgt. Meade Baker, Staff Sgt. Edward Vargo, Pvt. Stanley Gembala, Pvt. Herman Dunham, Jr., and other buddies were all killed in the landing. Bob Sales (Madison Heights, Virginia) landed with Capt. Ettore Zappacosta, the commanding officer of Company B, 116th Infantry. He was the only man in the boat team to survive. The captain was shot dead in the bloody water. Bob was ultimately knocked unconscious and temporarily evacuated. Thus, both commanding officers on Dog Green, along with almost all the boat officers, were dead within minutes of the landing. We were leaderless, except for our Col. Charles D. W. Canham, whom I never saw on Dog Green Sector, though he fought bravely.

In the midst of the leaderless carnage, I viewed a lone soldier coming up the beach from the east. He kept stopping and checking bodies on the sand. As he came closer, I discovered that it was Tech Sgt. Cecil Breeden, one of the three Company A medical aidmen. In my flashbacks in later years I would see this "angel of mercy" coming toward me. He was a five-foot, ten-inch, 180-pound, twenty-six-year-old man with a pleasant, mustached face. His relaxed nature made him fearless. Cecil was originally from Council Bluffs, Iowa, but made his home in Deer Creek, Colorado. On

Robert Sales, Company B, 116th Infantry, landed on Omaha Beach. He fought all the way to Germany and received the Silver Star on November 18, 1944.

Omaha Beach he was comforting the dying, saving the wounded, and helping some of us back into combat. At about 8:00 A.M., when I was taking cover behind the base of the wall (the tide was out), Cecil approached me. He knelt over me and started to clean my face wound. There was little he could do for me, except pour sulfur powder in the wound and pull my cheek back into place. He made me swallow twelve sulfa pills with water. As he was applying a bandage, shells started to rain down all about us. I reached up with my left hand, grabbing his shirt in order to pull him down to safety. Cecil slapped my hand away, saying, "You're hurt now. When I get hurt, you can help me." Cecil went through the entire European Theater Operation without a scratch. Incidentally, the bandage he applied to my face remained in place for more than thirty hours of combat. Cecil left me at about 8:15 A.M.—the last time I saw him on D-Day—to go help others. In fact, within the next hour, he dressed the right wrist wound of Colonel Canham, who continued to lead and fight. Even today when I think about Cecil, I envision a halo over his helmet. He must have injected me with some morphine, because I felt fuzzy-headed. In my mind and in the minds of those around me, Sergeant Breeden was probably the single greatest hero of D-Day.

Cecil had landed about 7:00 A.M. to the east of Vierville with a Company A Headquarters boat team. This boat was commanded by the executive officer (second in command) of Company A, 1st Lt. Ray Nance (Bedford, Virginia). In the boat with Ray and Cecil was Capt. Robert Ware, one of our battalion battle surgeons, and two other Company A aidmen. Ray received a bullet through his foot shortly after landing, and his war was over. Captain Ware (Virginia) was shot in the head as he exited the LCA, blood covering his red crew-cut hair. He had landed with this first wave without orders to do so, because he had been worried that the men would need his help. The two soldier combat medics were also gunned down. One of these fellows was Pvt. Tom Mullins, who had given me the aspirins on June 5.

With the tide out, about 9:00 A.M., the beach not only appeared red, but even the tide pools had red water in them. At about 10:00 A.M. on my Rima watch, I spotted Sgt. John Frazer (Company A, 116th Infantry) lying on the beach. He was lying parallel to the seawall. John's face was up, his eyelids moving, but he was not able to move off the beach. This six-foot tall, 190-pound Virginian had always been nice to me. I instinctively ran out to help him. As I knelt down beside him, with my left side facing the seawall, I placed my right ear next to his mouth. I thought he was trying to tell me something. A mortar shell exploded near-by. Three pieces of shrapnel penetrated the left side of my head, through the helmet. Placing my fingers of my left hand through the three holes, they came out saturated with blood. Blood streamed down the back of my neck as I clasped his right hand with mine. I pulled his right arm over my right shoulder. Then I crawled to the safety of the wall with him on my back. I left John behind the wall and did not see him again that day. John would have been hit in the face had my head not been there to absorb the shrapnel. Had I not gone to rescue him, he would have been blown up or drowned. In recent years, John related to me that he had passed out when I pulled him by his right upper extremity. He said he had a painful right shoulder wound.

While I was crawling with John on my back, my rifle, in my left hand, had been dragged through the sand, so at 10:30 A.M., I was cleaning the sand from my rifle bolt while taking shelter behind the wall. There were about four rows of dead and wounded in front of the wall, approximately forty soldiers who were being administered to by six soldier medics. These men had red crosses on their helmets and were from Company B, 104th Medical. One of them advised me to run down the beach to the east, to St. Laurent-sur-Mer, to be evacuated. I thought to myself, *Why not quit fighting?* I really didn't believe that I could ever be put back together. Also, I thought about Morris Saxstein, Robert Garbett, Jr., Hal Weber, Nicholas Kafkalas, Dominic Surro, and all my other slaughtered buddies. There was no way I was going to quit fighting. My job was to fight the enemy. But, feeling as if death was imminent, I prayed. I recited out loud the *Shema,* a Hebrew payer from Deuteronomy 6: 4-9. A prayer that I had learned as a child, it is the expression of a belief in one God and the keeping of His commandments. *Hear, O Israel! The Lord our God, the Lord is one.*

X

Vierville-sur-Mer

TWENTY-NINE, LET'S GO

About 11:00 A.M., Brig. Gen. Norman D. Cota, with a pistol in his hand, came running up our beach from the west. He was accompanied by a major I didn't recognize. I couldn't talk, due to my face wound, but some of the guys called to him to get down. It was reassuring to us to see this brave man on the beach, disregarding the snipers. We were advised that the only ones who were going to remain on the beach "were the dead, and those who were going to die." The call was "Twenty-nine, let's go," and we went.

Two hours later, one of our Sherman tanks, which had come in later in the morning, blew up near D-1. It was on fire as I joined a group of eleven other soldiers to ascend the bluff to fight. I call our group the "walking wounded," as all of them already had been wounded. I didn't know any of these soldiers, but most of them were probably Company B men. One of the fellows, with a tourniquet around his left arm, had his Twenty-ninth Division patch half blown off. There was blood dripping from his left hand and fingers, so he handled his M-1 rifle with his right hand. Another soldier, about six feet tall, had his right thigh bandaged. A short blond member of our miniature army, with a Virginian accent, was carrying a Thompson submachine gun and ammo. He was probably from the Ranger battalion that had landed at the Charlie sector, although I do not remember seeing a Ranger patch on his shoulder, which was covered with blood.

We worked our way up the bluff and headed for the west side of Vierville. There were trenches on our right side with dead German soldiers. The head of one of them had almost been shot off. He was probably the one I had shot earlier that morning with my armor-piercing bullet. At that point we were pinned down by machine gun fire coming from a house with a low stone wall around it. Probably due to my adrenaline, I was feeling remarkably strong for someone who had been wounded twice and hadn't had any food since the evening before. I had only fired one shot since 7:00 A.M., but a German soldier looked up from behind the wall, and I picked him off. One of our small, slightly built, red-headed men (with a right face wound) threw a hand grenade. The enemy fire ceased instantly. Eight of us were able to move on. The other four were not all victims of this fighting, but were incapacitated due to their previous wounds. We passed another house as we proceeded south. A French man and woman came out through the gate and were almost shot by us.

We had hoped to contact a larger group of Twenty-niners and join them. The objective of the 116th was to head west towards Pointe du Hoc. Soon we came under automatic gunfire from a nest of five German soldiers. One of our fighters got hit in the neck and died quickly. After about one hour, the skirmish was over and we had prevailed. I know I nailed one of the enemy. I was surprised to see how young these German soldiers were. Weren't we supposed to be fighting old men? Three of the enemy tried to surrender, but my guys were in no mood to take prisoners. At a Twenty-ninth Division Association national reunion in Ocean City, Maryland, in September 2000, I met Stewart Bryant, an associate member from Towson, Maryland. We spoke about this last little battle. He had been interviewing German veterans and knew exactly where it took place. The Germans told him that the five soldiers appeared to be victims of an airstrike strafing, the men were shot up so badly. I explained to him that our Ranger comrade, in a fit of anger, had emptied his submachine gun into them. I had had nothing to do with it. In fact, I was surprised that I was able to kill anyone. After that skirmish, there were seven of our walking wounded left. *Where were the rest of our guys?*

We reached a road stretching east and west. Running rapidly across the road, we hit the ground. I was crawling up to a low hedgerow when I felt a stinging in my left foot. It felt like a rock had hit the sole of my left shoe and a larger one had exited through the top. My canvas legging had a hole in the material that covered my shoe. It was now about 5:00 P.M., and I had just received my third wound on D-Day. Apparently, I had tripped some kind of "castrator" mine with my left foot. We had heard about them. It had fired a bullet through my left foot, instead of between my thighs. Leaning with my back against the hedgerow, I removed my left shoe. When I turned the shoe over, blood poured out like water from a pitcher. Utilizing my first-aid kit, I powdered the clean hole through my foot with sulfa. I proceeded to put on a good pressure bandage; however, just as I finished putting on a great dressing, we came under shell fire. I ripped off the dressing, pulled my shoe back over my bare, bleeding foot, and dove behind the hedgerow. My adrenaline was pumping, and I felt little pain. The seven of us remained there for a long time. Three of the fellows were smoking, which I couldn't understand, because I had never smoked. All of us wondered where the rest of our regiment was. We heard shooting and little explosions, but we didn't see anybody. It was getting dark, but the moon was exceptionally large and particularly bright.

Around midnight, shells started landing in front of us. We crossed to the north side of the road by 12:30 A.M. This turned out to be a disastrous move. We were ambushed by an MG42 from the left (west). All of us were hit. Since I was limping and bent over, I was shot through my left lip. Wound number one on June 7 was not a minor one. It took away part of my right upper jaw, teeth, and gums. Moving forward, I tripped over and fell on top of two of my buddies, but they could no longer complain. The others were moaning. One of the guys yelled, "Help me, Jesus." I expected the Germans to come down the road and finish us off, but they never came. I was all alone now: all my comrades were silent. I was prepared with my M-1 rifle and newly appropriated submachine gun to fight them, but I was in severe pain now from my face and my left foot, so I gave myself a small dose of morphine in the dorsum of my left hand. This produced relief of pain almost immediately, and some sleep. Before I dozed off, I heard the on/off sounds characteristic of the three German fighter planes flying over me. I could see their wing insignias. It was ludicrous, but I covered the luminous dial of my watch with my right hand. As I lapsed into semi-consciousness, the U.S. Navy started firing at them. It looked like Fourth of July fireworks. There I was, all alone with six dead buddies in a ditch, German soldiers down the road, enemy planes above me, and no other Twenty-niners around. *Did we lose the battle?*

I was apparently alternately sleeping and hallucinating between 1:00 A.M. and 3:00 A.M. In this dream state, I pictured a box of goodies sent by my mother, which I opened in Camp D-1. The homemade butter cookies, cake, and salami were shared with my Company A buddies. My buddies were cooking the green-mold-covered salami (from the long trip from the States) over an open fire, stuck on the ends of their bayonets. I thought I felt Garbett's presence. He was telling me how nice Newport News was but that he was going to live in Oxford, England, with his wife and child. I felt a hand on my left shoulder and heard a voice saying in broken English, "Don't worry Yonkee boy, everything will be fine."

My friend Stewart Bryant, while doing his research, interviewed the German veteran who ambushed us. He related that a German squad came down the road after 1:00 A.M. Seeing the seven apparently dead U.S. soldiers in the ditch, they searched the bodies for cigarettes. Stewart was told by these veterans that one of the men was alive. Thus, perhaps, one of these men had put his hand on my shoulder and spoken to me. I was not imagining it. Stewart also related that General Cota and some Twenty-niners came down that road later. He noted that there were "dead" GIs in the ditch.

At 3:00 A.M. I felt like I was dying. I was cold and clammy and had a "needles and pins" feeling throughout my whole body. I was awake, with no severe pain, even though I had been wounded four times in the last twenty hours. The last time I had eaten anything was more than thirty hours earlier. I kept drinking water from canteens that were no longer of any use to their owners.

85

XI

The Rescue and the Aftermath

WILL I BE MADE WHOLE AGAIN?

At about 3:00 A.M., while I was saying my last prayers, I saw an army ambulance approaching along the road from the west. It was silhouetted against the large, luminous moon. What was an ambulance doing west of my position? Was I seeing a mirage? I hadn't seen an ambulance in Normandy all day. Would I be able to stop it, if it was real? I couldn't yell at it, due to my mouth injury. Thus, I picked up the Thompson submachine gun, which I had never qualified to fire. Aiming above the ambulance, I fired a burst at it. It was really there, because two frightened GIs came out with their hands raised momentarily. I could not talk to them. They were angry but quickly sized up the situation. Noting that all the others were dead, they asked me, "Can you sit up in the ambulance?" I thought this was a very odd request, but I nodded affirmatively. Placing my arms over a shoulder of each, I limped to the back of the ambulance. When they had helped me up, I saw that the front of my uniform was soaked and dripped the blood of my dead fellow warriors. These men gave above and beyond and will never be cited for their bravery. I sat on the cold floor of the ambulance and fell backward from weakness. My helmet hit the steel floor. I heard one of the men say in a New York accent, "This guy just passed out." I was conscious, just weak from loss of blood and not eating. Why did they place me on the floor? Stewart Bryant told me that there had been a battle west of me while I had my two-hour morphine sleep. The ambulance was full of the battle casualties and already had wounded hanging on both its sides. I could not see this in the darkness. At any rate, my prayers were answered. In recent years, Dr. Joseph Shelley, M.D. (St. Augustine, Florida), commanding officer of the 104th Medical, advised me that he only had two ambulances on D-Day. One of them sunk in the English Channel.

I was taken down the beach, east of Vierville, near St. Laurent-sur-Mer. They laid me out on the sand in a stretcher with about eleven others. The army medics gave us water, blankets for warmth, and morphine for pain. Each injection was recorded on tags around our necks so that an overdose wasn't administered. I threw away the crumpled, waxy half-pound block of TNT I had in my left back trouser pocket.

At about 11:00 A.M. on June 7, German snipers fired at us from the bluff on my left front. One of our aidmen was shot through his Red Cross armband. What kind of heartless animals were those guys? Why would they fire at a Red Cross and defenseless, already-wounded men? They started killing the wounded. When they came to me, I was shot in the right knee. This was wound number five. Probably, the next bullet was aimed at my head. I knew they had telescopic sights. Miraculously, before I was fatally hit, a U.S. destroyer came in close to shore and bombarded their position on the bluff. I heard the *whisk* of their five-inch shells going over my head. After all the dust and smoke cleared, the snipers had been exterminated. Once more my number wasn't up. In recent years, when I spoke to some veterans in Alachua,

Florida, about D-Day, I met Glyn Markham. Glyn advised me that his destroyer, the *McCook*, blew away the snipers.

After four hours on the beach awaiting evacuation, I was carried by four U.S. Navy men, one of them a combat underwater demolition man, to a waiting LCVP assault boat. I was ferried out to LST 291 and hoisted up to the top deck by means of ropes. I was placed on the upper deck of this large ship. Looking up, I saw Old Glory flying above me. What a wonderful sight this huge flag was! After thirty-two hours of fighting, five wounds, bleeding, and not eating, my "longest day" was over. God had spared me. There were forty-nine hundred U.S. casualties on D-Day, and twenty-four hundred of them were on Omaha Beach.

From the deck of the ship, I was carried into a small operating room. There a young ensign physician and two corpsmen cut off my blood-drenched uniform, washed me, and administered plasma and glucose. The physician noticed that I was wearing an NYU football jersey under my army shirt. He told me that he had attended Columbia University. He mainly performed first aid, but he had to suture my right knee due to profuse bleeding. The left pocket of my shirt held my wallet with its family photos and two hundred French francs. They threw everything away. One of the corpsmen was attempting to remove my wrist watch, but I placed my right hand over it. Thus, my combat watch, with its leather band made by Robert Garbett, Jr., remained in my possession. It is now on exhibit in the National World War II Museum in New Orleans, Louisiana.

I spent four days on this ship, lying in a canvas bunk and listening to good music on the PA system. I have always loved music, but throughout my months of training and deployment, I had not heard any. As I began my treatments and during my long recovery, the music of my surroundings comforted me. Aboard the ship, all my treatment was administered by a navy corpsman who gave me penicillin and morphine by injection every four hours. He treated me with loving care and fed me clear soups and pineapple juice. But my time aboard was not free from the ongoing war's intrusions. Within my first two days aboard, the ship hit a mine. They had to land artillery, trucks, and tanks on the beach. Due to the damage caused to the propeller, we had to limp back to England.

In Normandy, we had had only medical aidmen administering first aid to the wounded, for our battle surgeon died trying to land with us. There were no helicopters, as in modern warfare, to evacuate the severely wounded rapidly. How many died because of this deficiency? Though unable to offer help to so many of our own soldiers, on-board the ship there were wounded German prisoners, many of whom were shipped to the U.S. before me. We even held a French traitor, a woman, aboard the LST 291.

When we arrived in Portsmouth, England, we anchored off the beach. I was placed in a stretcher on the floor of the ship's huge garage. A British medical officer, practicing triage, pointed his swagger stick toward me. Four British soldiers then transported me through knee-deep water past the ship's gigantic doors. I glanced back at the ship's bow, labeled LST 291. I will never forget that ship and the kind treatment afforded me by the crew. In later years, I was able to send a personal thank-you letter to each member of its crew. I wondered, *Did the British think that I was one of their men?* I was carried onto a beach and then placed in an ancient-looking British ambulance. Covered with a blanket, my compound-fractured left foot was continually being bumped. They took me to the British Royal Navy Hospital at Gosport Hants. The hospital had to obtain registration information from my dog tags, as I was unable to talk due to the extensive injuries to my mouth.

I was transferred on a gurney to a large surgical patients' ward. Commander Keating, a navy surgeon, and his staff gathered around the foot of my bed. The left cheek of my face was open, revealing teeth and gums lying on my tongue. My left foot was covered with green, gangrenous pus. I realize now that I had a pseudomonas infection in my foot. Thus, penicillin had been worthless against this type of bacteria. They had a corpsman take me to lab and x-ray.

After my x-rays, I was taken to the surgical suite. The British used chloroform for my anesthesia. I found out later that they worked three hours on me. Upon awakening from the anesthesia, I thought my left leg had been amputated because I could not feel it with my hand. Terrified, I started to cry. The sister, as the British nurses are called, removed my cover, revealing that I had been feeling a plaster cast. Attached to the cast, a metal cage covered my foot, with each toe strung up with wires. My face had also been operated upon. There were no longer teeth and gums lying on my tongue, though my left face and the roof of my mouth had to be left open, due to infection. When I drank fluids, they exited through my left nostril.

I have no words to describe how well the British treated me. The local English people visited and brought me flowers, fruit, and beer. The orderly assigned to me was a Jewish seaman. Seaman Sorkin made sure that I was not being "bumped" when transported from the ward, to lab, and to x-rays. British "wrens," or female sailors, bathed me. By administering appropriate doses of morphine, the sisters, or nurses, did not allow me to suffer any pain. They offered to write a letter to my parents; however, I wrote one in my own scribbled handwriting on June 12, 1944. I told them that I had a scratch on my face and foot, but I was otherwise okay. This letter was saved by my dear mother, along with others, and is now in one of my fourteen scrapbooks.

On June 24, two U.S. soldiers placed me in a stretcher and carried me to a waiting army ambulance. I had a very tearful farewell with my British caretakers. I was transported to the 250th U.S. Army Station Hospital in southeast England. At this hospital, I had a super nurse, Lieutenant Bodenschatz, from Goose Creek, Wisconsin. A new song, "Star Eyes," was serenading over the hospital's PA system. Later I found out that it was written by Don Raye and Gene De Paul and recorded by Helen O'Connell with the Jimmy Dorsey Orchestra for the movie *I Dood It*. Whenever I hear that song, I think of Lieutenant Bodenschatz's kind, loving treatment of me.

On June 26, I was taken to surgery. Prior to this surgery, I had refused to look in mirrors for fear of seeing how bad my face looked. Under sodium pentothal anesthesia, my left cheek and lip were primarily sutured closed. Coming out of this pleasant anesthetic, the new song "Skylark," which later I found out was written by Hoagy Carmichael and Johnny Mercer, and charted by Glenn Miller, was playing over the ward's PA system. I found momentary solace from my concerns as the strains of Glenn Miller, airing on the BBC, wafted around me.

On July 4, I was transferred by ambulance to the 158th U.S. Army General Hospital in Salisbury, England. I was placed in a large ward full of young, wounded soldiers, where at 5:00 P.M. daily, Glenn Miller's band could be heard on the ward's PA system. Many of the men in my ward had facial wounds. One of the soldiers, a Jewish kid from Brooklyn, New York, had his nose shot off. One evening, a young army captain visited me and pinned a Purple Heart medal on my pajamas. I was lying with my left leg up in traction and my face horribly scarred. It was still difficult for me to eat, drink, or talk. He said, as he saluted, "Son! Do you know why you are receiving this medal?" If it wasn't so sad, it would be considered hilariously funny. I did, however, have an understanding with him that the telegram sent to my folks would read "slightly wounded."

That was the only Purple Heart I received for my five separately inflicted wounds. Many soldiers receiving nothing more than a scratch or shaving cut were awarded a Purple Heart. Medals in World War II became used for "points" for a return trip to the States. If a soldier was an officer, or had an officer friend, he could be written up for a Purple Heart. Yet Cecil Breeden, my walking wounded buddies, and the boys from Bedford, were never properly cited for their bravery on D-Day. In 1945, I wrote a letter to Pres. Harry Truman about Cecil's brave actions. In 1990, I and many other Twenty-niners wrote to the senator from Colorado and the War Department in an attempt to obtain a well-deserved Distinguished Service Cross for Cecil. They advised us that an officer had to make the recommendation at the time his bravery was viewed. Cecil had dressed the right wrist of Colonel Canham on D-Day. However, all our outfit's officers were killed or wounded in the first few minutes on the beach. He did receive a couple of Bronze Star Medals and posthumously a commendation from the governor of Virginia.

The U.S. Army system of awards in World War II was flawed and has a very poor record, even in subsequent wars. Awards are very often given for political purposes, or as a reward for friendship by one officer for another. In the 2004 presidential election, one candidate was accused of writing up his own multitude of undeserving decorations. I cite, as another example, during the first three days of the Omaha Beachhead (June 6-9), twenty-eight men were awarded Distinguished Service Crosses. Of these, sixteen were officers, 50 percent with the rank of captain or higher. However, the men fighting beside me on Dog Green were

Capt. William Williams

mostly privates and corporals; the captains on my beach had all died, so there was no one to attest the bravery of the men who would later be awarded medals. The only Distinguished Service Crosses given for D-Day that I could prove valid were for Gen. Norman D. Cota, Col. Charles D. W. Canham, Capt. William Williams, 1st Sgt. Bill Pressley, and Sgt. John Roach, the latter three were from Company B, 116th Infantry.

I made attempts to obtain a cluster for my Purple Heart from the bureaucracy of the War Department for more than twenty years. Finally, I gave up in disgust. They advised me that an officer had to be present to witness each wound and its treatment. With all my officers dead, that request was ridiculous. I did receive the European Theater of Operations Medal with battle star and Invasion Arrowhead, American Theater Medal, Bronze Star Medal with Cluster, Combat Infantry Badge, Presidential Unit Citation, World War II

Sgt. John Roach

Victory Medal, Good Conduct Medal, and Expert Rifleman Medal. Gov. Thomas E. Dewey of New York presented me with the Conspicuous Service Cross of the State of New York.

The French have been very generous with medals, bestowing upon me the Croix de Guerre with Silver Palm, Medaille du Jubilee of Normandy, French Sixtieth Anniversary Badge, and many decorations and certificates from separate cities of Normandy. On May 30, 2005, I was awarded the Knight of the Legion of Honor by the president of France. The medal was presented at Florida International University in Miami on July 14, Bastille Day, by Consul General Brouchard. I spoke to the three hundred people present, thanking them for the award, and told them that when I returned to Normandy for the first time in 1988, I saw French schoolchildren decorating my buddies' graves with flowers, and I felt that everything was worthwhile.

While at the 158th General Hospital, my foot was pouring out so much green pus, my cast had to be removed. I had to soak my foot in potassium permanganate daily, turning my foot purple in color. The cast was later replaced, even though the infection was still present. I was now getting around on crutches, so they moved me out into a tent. Here I met two severely wounded Fourth Infantry Division soldiers. Anthony Boudreau was a twenty-four-year-old, short fellow from Vermont. He was married and had two young children. Tony had a hole in his right cheek and a smashed mandible. Steven Stefula, of Cliffside, New Jersey, also had facial injuries. His tongue was partly missing, and his entire chin, mandible, gums, and teeth were shot away. We became great friends. Since I had the only watch, I had to wake them up for Sunday morning mass.

Almost two months later, on August 21, I was transferred along with my new friends by plane to a hospital in Scotland. We landed at Renfrew and then were taken to the

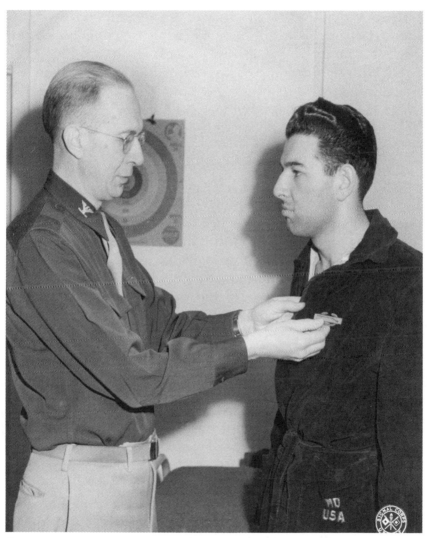

Baumgarten receives the Combat Infantry Badge, November 1944.

hospital in Glasgow, where we prepared for our long-awaited trips home. The Scottish people treated us kindly; a paperboy delivered a newspaper to me, but refused payment. Despite such kindness we were eager to board the plane for home.

Early on the morning of the twenty-fourth, we took off on our transatlantic flight with the Army Transport Command. We landed in the capital of Iceland for breakfast. I had real eggs and milk for the first time in almost a year. Then, we proceeded to cross the Atlantic in our four-motored Constellation. Though there were many wounded soldiers on the plane being flown back to the United States, I had four seats to stretch out on. The fellow behind me was horribly burned, scarred, and blind from the explosion of a white phosphorous shell. Some of the guys were in stretchers. There were two nurses tending to us. We landed in Gander Bay, Newfoundland, for lunch. When we took off for New York City, there was trouble with one of the engines. After a short, nervous delay, we were on our way to the States. We landed at LaGuardia Airport in New York City, my hometown, in time for dinner. With my left leg in a cast, there was no other way for me to disembark, so I had to dive out of the plane and was caught by four soldiers. The U.S. Customs personnel asked me if I had anything to declare. I replied, "my cast." Dinner was at Mitchell Air Corps Hospital in Long Island, New York.

Newly returned to America, I was advised by the physicians to call my parents and invite them to visit me. Bad mistake! My parents, sisters, brothers-in-law, nieces, and nephews all came to visit. Being on crutches, weighing about 110 pounds, my hair not yet grown in, my face grotesquely scarred, I was a stranger to them. They walked past me with no recognition. I enjoyed seeing them, but it was depressing to me to see their shocked facial expressions.

On August 27, my two buddies and I were flown to Massachusetts. We were taken by ambulance to Cushing General Hospital in Framingham, a new plastic surgery center. Cushing General was named for Dr. Harvey Cushing, a great neurosurgeon. It was a hospital made up of barracks attached by bridgelike ramps. When we arrived there, the three of us were emaciated. Our strength and weight had to be built up before any surgery could be performed on us. We were in such poor condition because we were not able to chew food. The staff at Cushing gave us rich milkshakes, ground-up steak, and even 3.2 percent beer. However, I was so weak that on one occasion, I went to the bathroom and fainted.

Capt. Murray Berger, the chief ear, nose, and throat surgeon, decided to use a new surgical procedure to close the fistula, or hole, between my mouth and my nose. He performed the Culdwall-loc operation on me in September 1944. Following this operation, fluids from my mouth no longer exited through my nose. Even though my face was still horribly scarred, I had no teeth, and I had to drag my left foot, I decided to go home for the Jewish New Year holidays, Rosh Hashanah and Yom Kippur. In the synagogue, I was given preferential seating up front; however, old friends and other parishioners looked away from me in horror. Before that experience, I would have found it inconceivable that I could be shunned and embarrassed because of my appearance. I learned a valuable life lesson at that time: to look beyond the superficial in my fellow man. People should show respect, regardless of physical features, race, ethnicity, or sexual orientation. This became invaluable in my later life as a physician.

In October 1944, Capt. Michael Lewin, destined to become one of the world's greatest plastic surgeons, operated on my face. He operated first on George Burr (Trumball,

George and Mrs. Burr

Connecticut). George's hand had been blown off almost completely, but Dr. Lewin managed to give George two opposing digits so that he could have a functional hand. George was discharged December 1944. He was able to use his repaired hand as a postal employee for over forty years. He gave me a 116th Infantry crest pin as a Christmas present. I still have it. George had landed with Company M, 116th Infantry, on Omaha Beach on D-Day, to the east of where I landed.

After Dr. Lewin repaired George Burr's hand, he operated on me for three hours. All my keloid scars were cut out and thrown away. Then the left side of my face was resutured with a multitude of fine stitches. My lip was rebuilt by Z-plasty and the use of mucous membrane. Facial scarring was reduced to a single diagonal one, in my shaving line. Then the dentists built for me artificial acrylic and steel plates to replace lost bone, gums, and teeth. By Thanksgiving, I was looking fairly normal. However, I still had to drag my left foot along, swollen, painful, and infected. The orthopedic surgeon, Dr. Sam Spadia, wanted to amputate part of my foot because it harbored osteomyelitis, an infection of the bone. I refused. Though not completely healed, I was now whole again, and looking human.

My stay at Cushing had its lighter moments, in addition to the serious surgical occasions. We found irony in the fact that the food in Cushing's cafeteria was served by German prisoners. We played ping-pong and basketball in wheelchairs and attended parties given by the people of Brookline, Massachusetts. There were USO show troupes that came to entertain us. One of the shows that impressed me starred George Jessel and the lovely Carol Landis. The girls of Wellesley College visited and wrote to us. Margerie Myers was one of these patriotic girls, and she visited me the evening of my plastic surgery. Soon after my surgery, with

Hal Baumgarten after extensive plastic surgery, Thanksgiving, 1944.

the sutures still in my face, the guys on my ward talked me into attending a hockey game at the Boston Garden, even though I felt very weak and sick that evening. Unbeknownst to me, the Boston newspaper printed a photo of us at the game. Dr. Lewin asked me the next morning, "Did you enjoy the game?" One afternoon, Colonel Isherwood, Cushing's CO, came to the ward and pinned the Combat Infantry Badge on my pajamas. I enjoyed this ceremony because all infantry soldiers consider this badge to be the highest award. It also came with a ten-dollar increase in salary, retroactive to D-Day.

By February 1945, I requested discharge. Though my buddies from England, Boudreau and Stefula, still needed extensive surgery, I was ready to resume my life. However, my condition was still considered poor. The lab found blood in my urine, and I needed additional oral and foot surgery. To expedite my discharge, I promised to go to the Veterans' Administration for follow-up treatments. I was discharged on February 12, 1945. My severance pay was three hundred dollars, a lot of money in those days. After registering my discharge paper at the Bronx County Court House, I returned to New York University on February 14, 1945.

XII

Chance Meetings

IT WAS MEANT TO BE

Before my discharge from the army in 1945, I had several chance encounters with family members of those who served in the Twenty-ninth. These meetings afforded me the opportunity to bring some level of comfort to the grieving families by sharing stories and information of their lost loved ones.

Mildred Weber, from Springfield, Massachusetts, decided to attempt to find out what happened to her brother Hal. The only information that she had was the telegram saying "killed in action." Hal had sent home a picture from Torquay, England, in March 1944. The letter sent with the photo stated, "The fellow in the picture is Pvt. Hal Baumgarten of New York City." Miss Weber called every Baumgarten in the New York City phone book. Finally, she located my father, who informed her that I was a patient at Cushing General Hospital. One of the saddest days of my life was having to talk to Hal's little four-foot, nine-inch mother and sister, Mildred. There was no way that I was going to reveal to them

```
Mr. Morris Baumgarten                           Aug. 11, 1944
Morris Baumgarten, Inc.
312 West 118th Street
New York 26, New York


Dear Mr. Baumgarten:

I am returning your clipping with this letter and, of course,
I cannot tell you how greatful we are to you for the interest
and help you have shown us.

We have already sent a letter to your son and although we can
not expect any miracle to happen, it will be just a little
satisfying if we can get just a little more information than
what we received from the War Department.

We are all happy to know that your son is living and though
he is and has suffered a great deal, some day soon he will
again be home with you.

Thank you again for the help you have been to us, we certainly
do appreciate it.

                            Very truly yours,

                            Mildred Weber
                            Mildred Weber
```

A letter from Mildred Weber seeking information about her brother Hal.

that his face had been blown away, so I spoke in general terms about D-Day. Hal's body has been brought home for internment in Springfield, Massachusetts. Mildred and Mrs. Weber are now deceased; however, Hal's nephew located me recently through the internet. I met Hal's brother, Austin, and his cute wife, Norma. They told me something interesting: Hal was apparently a Canadian citizen.

In November 1944, while waiting at the Tremont Street Bus Station in Boston, Massachusetts, a good-looking young girl approached and questioned me. She had noticed my Twenty-ninth Division patch on my overcoat. Then she related that her fiancé had been killed while serving in Company A, 116th. He was Pvt. Thomas Mullins, an aidman in Lt. Ray Nance's LCA.

Tom had given me some aspirin at about 9:00 P.M., June 5, on the *Empire Javelin*. I told her about Omaha Beach and what a great guy he was. She felt better knowing about the battle in which he had died.

In December 1944, the army gave me a leave pass for one month of "R & R" in Miami Beach, Florida, to visit my parents. My transportation was to be by plane. Unfortunately, it was snowing very heavily, and Boston's Logan Airfield was closed the day I was to leave. I had to trudge through the snow to the railroad station. After five hours, I arrived in New York's Grand Central Station. Eventually, I was able to catch a plane from LaGuardia to Miami. One evening after my arrival I went to the USO on First Street in South Beach (this area is part of the art-deco section of present-day Miami Beach). The Twenty-ninth Division shoulder patch on my "suntan" uniform stood out in this Army Air Corps-dominated area. A lovely young lady about six years my senior approached and questioned me about the Twenty-ninth. She wanted to know if I knew her husband, who was missing in action. Explaining to her how large the Twenty-ninth was, I asked her what outfit he was in. To my amazement, she turned out to be Bob Bleeker's wife. Bob was the company clerk of Company B, 116th Infantry. He had signed me into Company B on May 23, 1944, and given me a special pass to go to religious services. Sergeant Bleeker was a five-foot, ten-inch, ruggedly handsome 170-pound Jewish soldier from New Jersey. Five days later, Mrs. Bleeker phoned me to come over to her apartment. She had received his personal effects in a small, brown-paper-wrapped box. Among the items in the box were his smashed high-school graduation ring and a sheet of yellow French ration coupons. On the back of these coupons, under the

Coupon found with personal affects of Sgt. Bob Bleeker, company clerk, Company B, 116th Infantry, killed in Isigny, France. The company supply list is scribbled on the back.

words "Fermiers D'Isigny," was a list of supplies for Company B. Bob had been in the front lines with the company's men, assessing their needs. Isigny was about nine miles south of Omaha Beach. Bob Sales related to me in recent years, "Bleeker was blown to bits. He had no business being that far up front." I attempted to console Bob's widow, but it was difficult. What does one say to a bereaved wife? She gave me a few of the coupons for my scrapbook. We stayed in touch for a while after that meeting; in fact, I even dated her younger sister during my furlough.

One day my father introduced me to a very nice elderly couple from Fairfield, Connecticut. I told them about the death of Robert Dittmar on the beach, a boy from their hometown. Strangely, the organist in their church was Glea Dittmar, Bob's mother. They put me in touch with Glea, and we began a long, close friendship that lasted until her death in 1970. On our honeymoon in June 1949, my wife, Rita, and I visited Arlington National Cemetery. That is a heck of a place to take a new bride, but I wanted to take a photo of Bob Dittmar's gravestone for his mother. Glea had brought his body back from France but was too ill to visit the reburial site. I forwarded this picture to Glea. In return, Mrs. Dittmar sent us a ceramic "Bluebird of Happiness" for a wedding present. Her accompanying note stated, "Our relationship has been based on so much sadness, that this will serve to brighten things up."

In 1945, I answered an ad in the VFW magazine requesting information about Pvt. Robert Reece of Company A, 116th. I wrote to his mother in Buffalo, New York, and told her about our landing on the Dog Green sector. Bob had been killed, like others in Company A, in the swirling bloody waters on that beach. Mrs. Reece brought him back from Normandy for reburial in Buffalo.

In 1945, while I was attending New York University, I received a phone call from Pvt. Irwin Bogart from Silver Spring, Maryland. Irwin was the bazooka man in my old Company A boat team, #6. I thought everyone in that boat had been killed on D-Day. He was a six-foot tall, thin, young Jewish man with large lips and a very pleasant smile. The Company A records revealed that he was evacuated on D-Day but not wounded in action. Irwin was well liked in the outfit. Now he was a sporting-goods salesman, staying at the famous Plaza Hotel in New York City. We socialized around the "hot spots" in New York City for about one month. After that, I lost track of him. In 1999, while he was married and living in retirement in south Florida, we went to lunch together at

Worth Avenue in Palm Beach, Florida. Soon after that, he died from complications of diabetes.

In 2004, after I was interviewed on CNN, I received a phone call from Clarius Riggs' sister. She called from Pennsylvania to thank me for keeping her brother's D-Day story alive. However, in a friendly manner, she advised me that he was from Pennsylvania. I had said on television that he was from Tennessee. She also corrected my pronunciation of his first name. Riggs, the young man mowed down in front of me on D-Day, was buried in the Valley Forge National Cemetery in Pennsylvania.

All these contacts and meetings were meant to be. I lost contact with my hospital buddies, Boudreau and Stefula, in 1946.

XIII

Back to School

I HAD TO GET ON WITH MY LIFE

On February 14, 1945, I was back on the campus of the University Heights branch of New York University. In those days, the university had eighty-three thousand students, which made it the largest private college in the United States, though the Heights branch had less than three thousand all-male students. When people hear "New York University," they generally envision a big city campus with high-rise classroom buildings. This was not the case at the Heights. It was a beautifully planned country campus with wonderfully designed classroom buildings. Most of these buildings encircled a long, lovely landscaped mall. This mall led to a magnificent domed building, Gould Memorial Library, which, besides its great book collection, housed the most complete collection of timepieces in the world. Underground tunnels connected the campus buildings on each side. In the rear of these buildings was the Colonnade of Great Americans, with bronze busts and plaques of great Americans from varied endeavors: statesmen, scientists, and composers, among others. The campus had its own stadium, running track, tennis courts, gymnasium, and U.S. Army building with rifle range. The motion picture *A Beautiful Mind* showed the campus in one of its scenes. In other words, it was a marvelous school to return to, especially on the G.I. Bill.

Thus, I was back in the classroom studying biology, chemistry, and German. I was more fortunate than ninety-eight other students, who had made the ultimate sacrifice in World War II. Though in between semesters I would have to check into the Bronx Veterans' Administration Hospital for surgery, I did not miss any regular school days. I had an enormous hunger for learning and scored all As. College life was enjoyable, and I took part in all extracurricular activities on the campus. I was a sportswriter for the school daily newspaper and yearbook, the secretary of the honor society Perstare et Preaestare, and a member of the student council, where I fought for changes on the campus to benefit my classmates. I was elected president of the junior class in 1946. It was a great honor to find out that my fellow classmates held me in esteem. Our class prom was held at a famous New York nightclub, Billy Rose's Diamond Horseshoe.

I wanted to return to baseball and track, but I was suffering pain and swelling in my left foot. I settled for being a manager of the championship track team. Then, on March 17, St. Patrick's Day, I tried out for the baseball team. Coach Bill V. McCarthy welcomed me back. He had written to me while I was at Cushing. Some of the young guys wondered why this older, serious-looking fellow with a limp was given a place on the 1945 team. They found out during the first day of practice, when I hit a 450-foot line drive over the right center-field fence. For fear of getting hit on the left side of my face, I wore the newly designed "Dodger safety cap." The team used me as a bullpen catcher, pinch hitter,

Hal Baumgarten attending New York University, 1946.

Hal Baumgarten, New York University baseball team, May 1945.

and base-running coach. We won the Metropolitan Championship, playing teams like Fordham, Manhattan, St. John's, and CCNY. Also on our schedule were Rutgers, Yale, Columbia, West Point, and Annapolis. For my participation with the team, I was featured in my baseball uniform in an article in *Yank Magazine,* the U.S. Army's weekly periodical, on June 29, 1945 (pages 6-9). The purpose of the article was to encourage servicemen to return to college.

In September 1946, I purchased my first automobile, a 1946 Plymouth. I used the money that I had sent home from my army salary as well as my VA disability compensation. There was profiteering on the home front; I had to pay an extra five hundred dollars for the car. To try out the car, a college buddy and I took a short driving vacation to Canada. We drove straight up the eastern part of New York

State to Rouses Point, New York, then crossed over a bridge to Canada. We continued to Quebec, which is a wonderful replica of a French city. We had lunch at a beautiful hotel whose waterfall was used in one of Hitchcock's suspenseful motion pictures. As we traveled home, through the province of Quebec, we had breakfast at a farmhouse. The proprietors spoke Canadian French, and their menu was in French, but we had no problem communicating since I was fluent in French at that time. This trip was a nice break from the schoolwork and surgery.

I received my bachelor's degree in January 1947, slightly less than two years after my army discharge. Gen. Omar Bradley, commanding officer of the First Army on D-Day, was at my graduation as an honored guest. He congratulated me as he shook my hand. General Bradley, on D-Day, had refused to allow any reinforcements to land on Dog Green sector.

After graduation I decided to move to Miami Beach, Florida, where my parents lived. It became my home and was the first and only state in which I have ever voted. I applied for graduate school at the University of Miami, where I studied for a master of science degree in marine biology. My professor was a famous ichthyologist from Cuba, Dr. Luis R. Rivas. The college also made me a graduate assistant member of the faculty, and my name was listed as faculty in the 1948 University of Miami catalogue. As part of my assistantship duties, one day of every week was spent deep-sea diving in the south Atlantic Ocean. In order to receive my master's degree, I worked on a hypothermia thesis. Besides the individual research for my thesis, I also had to pass a test in a foreign language. German was the language that I chose.

In 1948, while I was studying on the beach, near the present South Beach art-deco area, a mutual friend introduced me to a gorgeous, sun-tanned University of Miami girl. Rita was wearing a one-piece black bathing suit. Also from New York City, Rita and I had much in common. She was destined to become the love of my life. The very next day, I was assigned to proctor a botany microscope exam on the main campus. I spotted Rita taking the exam and noted that she was having difficulty with one of the questions. I looked through her microscope and at her answer sheet, and laughed out loud. At the end of the exam, she inquired why I had laughed at her answer. I replied that the answer was a "bubble," and she had written a "spore." Rita said, "That was pretty rotten of the teacher to put an air bubble under the scope." I said, "I can see that you are very upset. Can I take you to lunch?" Her answer was, "May I bring a girlfriend?" After dating for one year, we were married at the Shelbourne Hotel on June 4, 1949. Rita, the mother of our three children, has been my best friend and lover for nearly sixty years.

After I received my M.S. degree, I taught in a private high school and worked part-time for the U.S. Post Office in Miami. In September 1951, the principal of Palm Beach High School offered me a position teaching biology and chemistry. My students would call me at home to tell me about animals they had caught, and they once brought me a live diamondback rattlesnake in a paper bag. As a teacher, I was also involved in aspects of the students' lives outside the classroom. The seniors at school held a senior-day picnic at Jupiter Beach, which the teachers had to chaperon. Another of my duties was to attend all their dances and proms. I also became that school's assistant football coach. It was a very rewarding experience. With Burt Reynolds, the future movie star, playing in our backfield, our team only lost one game in 1954.

Our first child, Karen Rae, was born at Good Samaritan

Hospital in 1952. My teacher's salary, even with an additional stipend for coaching, was not enough to support my small family, so I worked in the Palm Beach Summer Recreation Program. I was put in charge of a Recreation Park for the summer. My park had its own baseball team, comprised of children ages ten to thirteen, which I coached. The kids were taught how to bat, play their positions, slide, and steal bases. We played in a league of teams from other parks and did very well against these other teams.

West Palm Beach, Florida, was a terrific community to live in. We owned our own home on the south side of town and had a good social life. I went to evening meetings during the year at the Masonic lodge and the local VFW chapter, where I was elected commander. I was also the principal of a large Sunday school. Rita and I spent time with a group of about a dozen young couples our age. Each of us would trade off hosting super house parties with food and drink. Every holiday was celebrated with our group. We would rent hotel conference rooms for our socials, like on Halloween. In the summer, we all had cabanas at Palm Beach so that we could enjoy the sun and sea. The men would play four-wall handball, and I had a regular Sunday tennis game. The children enjoyed swimming in the pool.

During the summer of 1955, I spent my entire vacation in the Biltmore VA Hospital in Coral Gables, Florida. I needed two more operations on my bad left foot. One of my toes had to be amputated. While a patient in the hospital, I met Mark Wynn. Mark had been one of my students in a comparative anatomy lab at the University of Miami. He visited me everyday because he now was working in the hospital's lab. Mark was going to enter the new University of Miami School of Medicine in September. Handing me an application for medical school, he said, "You were meant to be a doctor." In discussing it, he refused to accept any of my excuses, though I protested, "I am too old," and "I have a wife and child." He was four years older than I and married with four children. Rita encouraged me to apply and said, "When they reject you, you will get it out of your system." Thus, I took the medical aptitude test, and aced it. The School of Medicine accepted me immediately in January 1956. We had to sell our home and obtain another one in Miami. I had to sadly tender my resignation to the Palm Beach County schools.

While at Palm Beach High, I had developed a great bond with my students. I had formed a biology club for about fifty students. The club had our own insignia and we met after school hours, discussing science, earning money for projects, having our own socials with dancing, and taking field trips. For our socials, we rented a recreation building from the city. One of our field trips was to Vero Beach's McKee's Jungle Gardens, a seventy-mile trip. I was also in charge of the school's science fair every year. The projects brought in by the students were excellent. All of this activity was voluntary on my own time, with no monetary compensation; however, I loved the kids, and I would miss them.

I also had cultivated a level of respect among my peers in the school system. In the pre-school meetings of the Palm Beach County teachers, I always led the Pledge of Allegiance. The superintendent of the Palm Beach County schools put me in charge of all of the science teachers in the county. I hated to give all this up.

Not only was saying goodbye hard, we were having a difficult time trying to sell our home. The equity in our home was necessary to help finance medical school. Finally, we decided that if we didn't sell the house that week, we would give up on our Miami dream. A reverend from the Church of God miraculously appeared and purchased our home with cash.

Medical school was demanding, but my grades were

excellent. My classes for the first two years were held in the stables of the Biltmore Hotel, a VA hospital in Coral Gables, Florida. The school was the first accredited medical school in the state of Florida. The training at the University of Miami School of Medicine was very rigid, but great. In the freshman year, fourteen students flunked out. Nine students were dropped in the sophomore year. During the final two years, five more bit the dust.

The subjects I studied my first year were biochemistry, cytology, bacteriology, physiology, and anatomy. My introduction to anatomy was in the dissecting lab. Here there were cadavers on gurneys, covered by white sheets. Four students were assigned to each cadaver. When the sheets were removed, they revealed embalmed human beings. Though it was the best way to learn, this was a shock to many of the students, who became ill. I was accustomed to seeing dead bodies from D-Day. We discussed and dissected one organ system at a time and studied from x-rays. We had to get used to the smell and the touch of embalming fluid; the carbolic acid would make your fingertips feel numb and tingly. On going home after the day's classes, we would be on "autopsy call." One evening, when I was sitting down to have dinner, I was called to go down to the Jackson Memorial Hospital morgue. After driving twenty miles, I had to observe an autopsy on a newly dead person. Each week we would have classes at Jackson Memorial Hospital and examine patients with various ailments. I was assigned a project—to research our cadaver's history. It was difficult to do without a computer, but I determined that he was seventy-three years of age and had died as a result of a ruptured spleen. A policeman had struck him on the left side while he was sleeping on a park bench. When we got into his abdomen, we viewed a tremendous amount of dried blood on the left side.

My courses were difficult and I had to study around the clock to maintain my high grades. However, our second child, Bonnie Sue, was born in my sophomore year. Thus, I couldn't have been studying all the time. Even though I had an exam the next morning, I helped deliver Bonnie. In my junior year, I was on the obstetric service. I personally delivered fifty babies. What a thrill! Also in my junior year, I had to do all the lab work on assigned new hospital patients. Even though the hospital's lab did the work at the same time, our lab work proved to be more accurate. In our senior year, we operated on dogs to practice surgical procedures. The animal became your patient and was kept in good health. We also treated patients in psychiatric and family practice clinics. I received my medical degree in June 1960, but my sweet mother, who had died on May 23, 1960, had not been able to see the degree bestowed.

I received my internship training at Mount Sinai Hospital in Miami Beach. I would arrive very early in the morning and wait for a specialist to accompany me on the rounds. This was a great learning experience. When I was on emergency room duty, there were many amazing experiences, such as exchanging incompatible blood in a newborn, and the very often near-fatal heart attacks, but I recall one experience in particular. I was called to the scene of an auto accident on First Street. A man was slumped down in the passenger seat of a Cadillac convertible. He was cold and clammy and had an ashen coloration, his blood pressure was very low, and his pulse was thready. The left abdomen was tender. I diagnosed a ruptured spleen. Our ambulance had to traverse more than forty streets in order to get back to the hospital, with much cross-street traffic to contend with along the way. I had the Miami Beach Police Department block off every street to the hospital. At the same time, I started an IV and radioed the hospital to have a surgeon and surgical suite prepared for an emergency splenectomy. We raced to Mount Sinai at eighty miles per hour, siren blaring, and got him into surgery. The result was a live and appreciative patient.

I wanted to be a general practitioner because I enjoyed every phase of medicine. There was no doubt in my mind that God had placed me in the correct profession. We moved to Jacksonville, Florida, where I practiced as a GP and industrial surgeon for forty years. In 1963, I passed a two-day exam and became a Board Certified Charter Fellow of the American Academy of Family Physicians. In order to maintain this membership, I had to take a board exam every six years. This board certification did not affect my fees, which I kept 30 percent lower than my local colleagues.

In August 1984, I became the medical director of the Gulf Life Insurance Company, a subsidiary of the American General Life Insurance Company. This I did while still maintaining my own private practice. Once each year, the company sent Rita and I to some fabulous meetings in the U.S. and Canada. At these meetings, with individuals from all over the world, we met some very nice physicians and their wives. Two physicians we met on these trips, Charles Jones and Bob Ferguson, became good friends. We traveled to Phoenix, Minneapolis, Seattle, New York City, and Toronto and Quebec, Canada. In addition to the great social opportunities, these conventions allowed me to enhance my medical knowledge. In many ways, insurance medicine was way ahead of the medicine learned at our local hospital meetings because I learned about special CT scans and echocardiograms as well as how to identify certain ailments from lab work before these methods were commonly used in the hospitals at home.

Gulf Life left town in 1991, and I spent my final six years of practice working part-time with the Veterans'

Administration. Here I was able to treat disabled veterans, most of whom gravitated to me. I received in a ceremony a large framed Certificate of Meritorious and Conspicuous Service to Veterans from the national commander of the Military Order of the Purple Heart. In 1996, I was elected national surgeon of the Twenty-ninth Division Association. Thus, becoming a physician was the second reason that God saved me on D-Day. The first, and primary reason, was to be the spokesman for the true heroes of D-Day, the ones I left lying face down in the sand. Having fulfilled my purpose to help save lives as a physician, I now must keep the D-Day story alive.

XIV

Reunions

THEY WERE STILL ALIVE

After the war, I became active in the VFW (Veterans of Foreign Wars), DAV (Disabled American Veterans), and MOPH (Military Order of the Purple Heart). My membership with these organizations provided me the opportunity to interact with my fellow veterans and share our stories of survival. I served as the commander of the DAV in Miami Beach, Florida. During my time in that capacity, I became the aide de camp to Gen. Jonathan "Skinny" Wainwright, the national commander of the DAV. I had lunch with this famous general, who had surrendered Corregidor in 1942. We rode around in a Florida Highway Patrol car while he related to me the tortures he endured at the hands of his Japanese captors. We went deep-sea fishing together. A strong man, he showed me where his ribs had been broken and nail beds burnt to try to make him give up information.

Some of my activities with the VFW and DAV allowed me to take celebrities to the Biltmore VA Hospital to entertain the veterans. One of the great stars was Sophie Tucker, the "last of the red hot mamas." While visiting and entertaining the vets, she fell and broke her ankle. Like a true trooper, she continued her visit with a plaster cast on. She also donated a lot of money to my local veterans in need.

Though active in the veteran community all this post-war time, I had ignored the Twenty-ninth Division Association because I thought all the guys I knew were dead. However, I decided to go to Normandy with the Twenty-niners in September 1988 to dedicate a monument in the city of Vierville-sur-Mer. At Dulles Airport, I found out that many of the D-Day veterans of the Twenty-ninth were still alive. I met John "Bob" Slaughter of Roanoke, Virginia, a six-foot, five-inch, rugged sixty-three-year-old hero of Company D, 116th. Bob not only survived the landing, but also finished the war in Germany. Wounded on two separate occasions, this was no easy task. He later became the director of the National D-Day Memorial Foundation and was instrumental in its opening in Bedford, Virginia, on June 6, 2001. I have corresponded with Bob Slaughter by letter and phone ever since our airport meeting.

At the airport, I also met Lucille Bogess from Bedford, Virginia. She was the kid sister of Bedford and Raymond Hoback, who died on D-Day. As mentioned, Bedford was killed by shrapnel from the same shell that hit me. Raymond's body was never found; however, a soldier from West Virginia found his family Bible on the Dog Green sector of beach on June 7 and mailed it to the Hobacks.

While on the Pan Am airbus to France, I asked Bob Slaughter, "Is there a Cecil Breeden on the plane?" He advised me to look for a fellow wearing a cowboy hat on the other side of the plane. I ran to the other side of the plane and tapped that man on his left shoulder. The same face that I remembered leaning over me on D-Day turned and gazed up at me. Though he was thinner due to open-heart surgery,

Hal Baumgarten and Sgt. Cecil Breeden.

and his moustache and hair had a sprinkle of gray in it, the same pleasant, smiling face was there. We embraced, both having thought the other to be dead. Cecil related to my wife what my face had looked like on D-Day. Cecil and I wrote to each other until he died of a ruptured aortic aneurysm on May 23, 1991. May 23 has a lot of significance for me. I was transferred into Company B, my mother died, and my son Hal was born on May 23. Cecil had instructed

125

his girlfriend to write to me after his death. In her letter she expressed his warm feelings for me. I wrote a fitting epitaph for Cecil in the Twenty-ninth Division Association's quarterly journal.

Together the survivors of the Twenty-ninth finally returned to Normandy. A lunch was served before the dedication of the Twenty-ninth Division Monument in Vierville. It was eerie that the restaurant was located on the road where I had almost died. Present in the restaurant were the mayor and some of the townspeople. We tanked up with lots of wine and calvados for our expected sight of Dog Green sector. It would be my first sight of the beach in forty-four years. Looking at the water reminded me of our landing on the boat. I remembered all the horror viewed on D-Day, including blown-up landing craft, dead bodies, and red channel water. It was impossible to stop crying. Walking down the beach to where I had landed, I noticed the twenty-five-foot seawall was no longer there, though the pillbox on the right flank was still present, staring out from the bluff like a Cyclops. No longer was the low seawall in front of Vierville covered with loose shale stones; it was now covered with a layer of cement. There were steps built into the seawall for the tourists.

The dedication ceremony was very memorable. A French Foreign Legionnaire band was stationed to the left of the flag-covered monument. Behind our monument were the fighting French of World War II, with their battle flags. On the right side of the monument were twenty-nine soldiers of the Maryland National Guard, along with the governor of Maryland, who had sent them. Also present were officers and soldiers of the active Twenty-ninth Division Light, as well as their commander, Gen. Boyd Cook. The "Star Spangled Banner" and "La Marseillaise" were played with the raising of the respective flags. The

Hal with Cecil Breeden in front of a pillbox at the D-1 entrance, September 1988.

Hal in front of WN 71 pillbox, September 1988. Arrow marks location Hal landed on D-Day.

Pillbox on the right flank of Omaha Beach whose guns killed so many Twenty-niners on D-Day. Note bluff on right side (north), shielding it from naval fire.

flag-raising was followed by dramatic invocations and speeches by French and U.S. generals. Dignitaries from both countries also spoke. The monument was finally unveiled, and each of us placed a rose at its base. Along with divisional citations and battles fought, a poem is inscribed upon it:

> From the North and the South in our land we came that free-dom may prevail. On D-Day, 6 June 1944, in the great allied amphibious assault, the 29th Infantry Division stormed ashore on Omaha Beach to win a beachhead. Our fallen lie among you. They gave the last full measure of their devotion. Sleep, comrades for-ever young. We salute you. Remember us.

This edifice stands in the center of the town, significantly looking down at the beach below.

After the dedication, we visited the Normandy American Cemetery and Memorial at Colville, with its approximately ninety-four hundred crosses and Stars of David. Each one faces west toward the U.S. There would have been many more graves, but many families brought their loved ones' remains home. I visited the grave of 1st Lt. Harold Donaldson but couldn't find Robert Garbett, Jr.'s cross. The cemetery's director told me that his body had been shipped home. Looking upon my return home for his place of burial, I was able to eliminate Oxford, England, and Arlington, Virginia. Writing to the mayor of New Port News, Virginia, I was informed that his family no longer lived there, nor was he buried there. However, she did mail me a book with the picture of their Memorial Arch to Veterans. His name was inscribed on the wall of the arch. Bob would have liked that. While in the American cemetery, there were no dry eyes.

I saw French schoolchildren placing flowers on American graves, a very comforting and touching gesture. The French people in Normandy love Americans and bring their children up to love us. This love affair between the two countries dates to the American Revolutionary War, when a French nobleman, the Marquis de Lafayette, risked his life, reputation, and fortune to fight with us for our freedom. When I attended college, our Colonnade of Great Americans had a separate but adjacent section with a bust and plaque honoring him. As I landed on D-Day, I had said to myself, "Lafayette, we are here."

We visited Le Mémorial de Caen, a museum of the Battle of Normandy in Caen, a magnificent memorial to all who fought in Normandy and the European campaign. Students and tourists from all over the world visit this memory- and artifact-filled museum. Our visit took us to Saint-Lô, a city that to capture cost the Twenty-ninth Division seven thousand casualties and a multitude of local civilian deaths. Maj. Thomas P. Howie, of the First Battalion, 116th Infantry, the major of Saint-Lô, was killed just outside the city. By order of Gen. Charles Gerhardt, the commanding officer of the Twenty-ninth Division, his flag-draped body on a jeep led the 116th into the city. It was placed on the rubble from the only building standing, Saint Mary's Church, which had lost one of its steeples in the bombardment. The mayor had a champagne reception for us at the city hall, followed by a luncheon. We decorated the Major Howie Monument and a monument for the citizens of Saint-Lô with wreaths and heart-stirring ceremonies. The mayor was a physician and took us to visit the 550-bed American Regional Hospital. Due to donations from our division, this hospital had the Twenty-ninth Division insignia in its lobby and on many of its rooms' doors. Here we were wined and dined again. To culminate our trip, we had a huge banquet in Bayeux. Throughout the trip, the French people hugged and kissed us and requested autographs.

The 1988 trip to Normandy was an eye-opening experience

Hal Baumgarten and Cecil Breeden at Colville American cemetery wreath-laying, September 1988.

for me. Though I had discovered that not all my D-Day buddies were dead, looking at the graves of the men who had landed with me, I realized that they could no longer speak. I had the responsibility to tell their story. This realization has shaped my later life and led me to my many speaking engagements and radio and television appearances.

In 1990, I attended a Company B reunion in Madison Heights, Virginia. It was held at the home of Bob Sales. This huge six-foot, six-inch Twenty-niner had landed with Captain Zappacosta in the Company B command boat on D-Day as the captain's bodyguard and SCR radioman. He was the only man who survived from that boat team. This Twenty-ninth Division hero continued to fight all the way to Germany, where he almost lost his life. He received a Silver

Star on November 18, 1944. After a long hospitalization, he was discharged with only one eye. Upon returning home, he designed in his front yard what he called a "Garden of Heroes," a memorial stone with bronze plaque listing the names of our fallen Company B buddies.

A plaque was presented the day of our reunion to the family of Sgt. Clarence "Pilgrim" Roberson. I hesitantly related to them how he died on D-Day. They were happy to find out that he had prayed his rosary before dying.

Attending this meeting was Charles Conner, of Charleston, West Virginia. After speaking with Charlie, I realized that he was with me in Boat Team #1 on D-Day. He had exited the boat to the left and wisely taken cover behind one of the two tanks on the beach. As the tank came under shellfire, he swam to the other one. Ultimately, he was able to work his way to the seawall, the Vierville Draw, and up into Vierville. After eating some hard bread and drinking milk provided by the local people, his "longest day" was over; however, in the early afternoon, he had been able to help capture twenty Germans. On June 13, he was severely wounded near Isigny. Since our first meeting, we have corresponded regularly. Charlie sent me a cap inscribed "the longest day," which I wear and treasure.

Also present at that meeting was a quiet Southern gentleman named Harlow. This Company B veteran from Madison Heights, Virginia, used his own handkerchief on D-Day, and one borrowed from General Cota, in order to semaphore the battleship *Texas*. The battleship then knocked out a pillbox that was holding up the advance. He was never decorated for that outstanding feat, even though the general was right next to him and witnessed his action.

I also met Bill Pierce of Company B. This gray-haired, rugged, intelligent man had more knowledge of our company than anyone. He should have written a book about

Company B, but he passed away before beginning such a project.

John Roach (Panama City, Florida) was there as well. Although wounded in the hand on D-Day, as a Company B sergeant, he kept fighting. He helped knock out a pillbox on Dog Green sector and earned a Distinguished Service Cross. He was in Vierville by midnight. He passed away in 1991.

First Sergeant Bill Presley of Company B was missing from our reunion because he had recently died of a heart attack. Bill had been a ruggedly built six-foot, four-inch-tall 240-pound man. He was able to get past the beach on D-Day rapidly and was in Vierville by midnight. While going up the bluff toward Vierville, he spotted a battery of German 105 mm mortars. They were firing at the men on the beach. Sergeant Presley took a radio from a dead navy forward observer and radioed the U.S. destroyer *Saterlee*. With his directions, they were able to wipe out the German position. He earned a Distinguished Service Cross for his valor.

On June 6, 1991, I attended a Company A reunion in Bedford, Virginia. Ray Nance, who was second in command on D-Day, took Rita and I sightseeing. We visited the Bedford County Courthouse. On the front lawn of this building is a memorial stone in memory of the twenty-three men from Bedford who died fighting in Normandy, twenty-one of those deaths occurring on D-Day. I knew seventeen of them personally. This stone was a gift from France and was dedicated by a French admiral. We visited the cemetery of this tiny town, which had sacrificed so much for the winning of the war. I visited the graves of Capt. Taylor N. Fellers, commanding officer of Company A, and 1st Sgt. John Wilkes. Sergeant Wilkes was a huge, red-haired, freckle-faced man who was shot through the head on D-Day. I also sadly viewed Frank Draper's grave in that cemetery.

At our reunion dinner, I was invited to light a candle in memory of Cecil Breeden, who had died that year. I couldn't help but express to the group my feelings about this great hero. At this dinner, my buddies John Barnes, Russell Picket, and Roy Stevens were present. These three, although unable to land on D-Day, received their Purple Hearts later. Roy Stevens had a twin brother, Ray, who was killed on the beach on D-Day.

In 1992, I attended a "reenactment of D-Day ceremony" on Lake Pontchartrain, in New Orleans, Louisiana, sponsored by the Eisenhower Center of the University of New Orleans. Dr. Stephen E. Ambrose, the director, was very kind to introduce me that day to the thousands of honored guests and people of New Orleans. I did not realize at that moment that he was going to have a great influence on my life. Dr. Ambrose became my good friend and mentor. He is, no doubt, the greatest American historian of the twentieth century and lobbied for the building of and raising of funds for the National World War II Museum, which opened on June 6, 2000.

On Labor Day weekend in 1992, I attended my first Twenty-ninth Division Association national reunion. This meeting was held in Roanoke, Virginia. At this event, I had the honor of meeting Joseph Balkoski, author of *Beyond the Beachhead*. His book is an outstanding work of historical literature. In the course of conversation, I related to him my search for Robert Garbett's burial site. His face lit up and he said, "Recently, while walking through the National Cemetery in St. Augustine, Florida, I saw that name on one of the headstones." He remembered it because he was surprised to find a Twenty-ninth Division grave in Florida. This was incredible. St. Augustine is a thirty-minute drive from my home. I had been visiting that town regularly for more than thirty years. Rita and I had had dinner there within the

Robert Garbett, Jr.'s grave in St. Augustine, Florida, National Cemetery. He was killed in action on D-Day.

previous two weeks. The day after the reunion ended, I drove to the cemetery and found Bob's grave. The cemetery's historian, Mr. Hawks, advised me that Bob's father had moved from Maryland to nearby Gainesville, Florida. He brought Bob's body back from France to be interred close to him in St. Augustine. Looking down at his grave brought back memories of him. I prayed and placed a stone on his cross. Sadly, I was never able to locate his wife and child.

The 1993 national reunion of the Twenty-ninth Division Association was held at Bainbridge, Massachusetts. We held our Sunday memorial service in the famous Old North Church in Boston. I was very impressed with the Massachusetts State Highway Patrol escort for our buses from our hotel into Boston. This church, from the days of

Paul Revere, has been an amazing place to pray. The square in front of the church was cordoned off by the Boston Police Department so that we could dedicate it to one of our deceased 115th Regiment comrades. At the close of this unforgettable ceremony, we sang "God Bless America" in the square.

Having attended all these meetings, as well as the Florida Post #2 meetings annually in Punta Gorda, Florida, I realize what a great "family" of fine human beings I have been blessed to be in fellowship with. Through my correspondence and interaction with my fellow veterans, I have found out where several others were at the end of their "longest day." Harry Parley, Company E, 116th, landed at H-Hour, the hour our landing commenced on D-Day, near Easy Red sector. He is one of my fellow New York Jewish buddies. Carrying his bulky flamethrower, he landed under heavy fire. After fighting his way up the bluff inch by inch, he and his remaining buddies made it to the top. That evening, he was too tired to dig a deep foxhole and fell asleep back to back with one of his buddies. John Robertson, Company F, 116th, from Jacksonville, Florida, landed on the Fox Red sector under heavy enemy fire. He was carrying heavy mortar shells and was almost run over by a U.S. tank. His evening was spent at the top of the bluff with his buddies who were still alive. From New York City, Sergio Maddelena, Company F, 116th, landed with Robertson. He too was lucky to spend the evening at the top of the bluff. Ray Scheurer, Company C, 116th, was supposed to land on my bloody sector; however, Company C landed way to the east in the First Division's sector. Company C was the only 116th outfit to land intact on D-Day. Ray (Kenilworth, New Jersey) was one of their few men to get wounded, receiving a severe ankle wound going up the bluff. He still limps today. The men from Company C went up the bluff and helped capture Vierville from the south side. Thus, their mistake in landing was very fortuitous. It was of great interest for me to find out where my fellow Twenty-niners were located when I was alone on D-Day.

XV

Guilt

WHY ME?

During my hospitalization following combat, I had horrible nightmares and flashbacks. I would wake up shouting "Get down!", recalling the moment when Sgt. Clarence Roberson was praying on the beach. Many of the sights I viewed on D-Day were repressed in my subconscious. Gradually, over the years, small amounts of these horrific memories leaked out from the depths of the dark canals of my brain. Often, when I look down at the surf on Jacksonville Beach, I flashback and the water appears red with blood. These are very frightening occurrences. Driving behind a diesel bus and inhaling its fumes often triggers me momentarily to flashback to the assault boat on D-Day. What horrific remembrances of D-Day, the water, the high waves, the cold, and the floating vomit in the boat!

One vivid flashback occurred after my first conversation with John Frazer in 1990. I had asked John why he had been lying on his back without trying to move off the shell-pounded beach. His reply was, "Didn't you notice that both of my legs were shattered?" Afterward, in my dreams, I could vividly picture his blood-drenched uniform trousers. I had lunch with John in 1996 in Fort Myers, Florida. He related that he had passed out when I pulled his injured right arm over my right shoulder so that I could crawl with him on my back. My main thought, at the time, was to get him off that beach. I tried to block out as much of the bloodshed as I could.

While a patient in Cushing General, I did not dare reveal these weird happenings. In World War II, one would be labeled as a "Section 8," severely battle fatigued, or "psycho." Now it is referred to as posttraumatic stress disorder. During World War II they would have placed me in a psychiatric ward, with all its bad connotations. I did not desire that stigma on my record, which would have affected my future educational goals.

Only in 1993 did I seek help. All these years the major theme of my flashbacks was based on guilt. Why did I survive, when so many others died? I found it very difficult to talk to some of my deceased buddies' family members. I thought they were thinking, "It should have been my brother or husband to have lived." I attempted to rationalize my guilt. Could my survival have been due to my prayers? These thoughts could not be completely true. Our Catholic chaplain, Father Kelly (New Britain, Connecticut), died on the beach, and Raymond Hoback had probably prayed from his family Bible on the beach. The psychiatrist at the Veterans' Administration advised me to take an antidepressant medication. When I asked him if the pills would cause my nightmares to disappear, he replied, "No . . . but it will make you sleep better." Thus, I take no medication at this time.

Over the years, I am beginning to realize that God had a job in mind for each of us survivors. My Company A buddy John Barnes was to teach high-school English and social studies for thirty-three years. His work was in Holland

Patent, New York, where he stimulated young minds. He also served as mayor of his town for six years. David Silva of Company D, 116th, who was wounded on D-Day, and Patrick Gilluly of the Twenty-ninth Division Engineers both became Catholic priests. Father Silva has done much good over the years, ministering to his people in Ohio. Father Gilluly took care of his parishioners in Beckley Springs, West Virginia. Both of these gentlemen are now retired. These are just a few of the Twenty-ninth Division survivors of whom I am proud.

I was to become a physician. During my practice of medicine, sick people never needed an appointment to see me night or day. My fees were always 30 percent lower than my local colleagues. Many of my diagnoses saved lives. For example, I discovered early cancers, melanomas, and acute intestinal diseases in my patients. Even when I sutured wounds very little scarring remained. I helped alcoholics on a straighter path. I know I made a difference in peoples' lives. Comforting the sick and dying was probably part of God's plan for me. He helped guide my hands, my heart, and my head.

The guilt of survival will no doubt haunt me till the day I die. My consolation is that God spared me in order to help my fellow man. We are all destined to fit into some unique niche in the master plan of our Creator.

XVI

The Fiftieth and Fifty-fifth Anniversaries of D-Day

YEARS GO BY

The fiftieth anniversary of D-Day was a very momentous event in the United States, as well as in other parts of the world, and I took an active part in the celebrations. In front of the Capitol, Charles Durning, a famous character and Academy Award-winning actor, dramatically related my D-Day story, quoting from my book *Eyewitness on Omaha Beach, June 6, 1944,* on National Public Television as part of the national Memorial Day program. This was on the evening of May 29, 1994. Gen. Colin Powell, the army chief of the general staff, said that my story was "poignant." My local newspaper, the *Florida Times-Union,* wrote about John Robertson and I returning to France for the fiftieth anniversary. We were also interviewed on our local television channel. Bob Edwards, from National Public Radio's *Morning Edition,* broadcast his interview with me on NPR on June 6, 1994. *People* magazine interviewed and photographed me for their May 29, 1994, issue, and *USA Today* photographed me and wrote about my D-Day adventure. I purchased the *USA Today* paper with my article while I was in Normandy,

France. My picture and story made the front and magazine sections of all the Knight-Ritter newspapers in the U.S., such as the *Los Angeles Times, Miami Herald,* and *Detroit Free Press.* All this unsolicited publicity was somewhat embarrassing, but it helped keep the D-Day story alive.

On June 5, while in Saint-Lô, France, I was interviewed on CNN's *Night Edition,* with Frank Sessno. He sent a limousine to transport me from Saint-Lô to the American cemetery at Colville. He interviewed Bob Slaughter and I on the same program as he did Pres. Bill Clinton. The filming took place in the American cemetery, so when I was asked what was so meaningful to me, I was able to point to the stars and crosses and reply, "I don't want these buddies to ever be forgotten." Mr. Sessno also asked me who my favorite general was on D-Day. My unhesitant answer was, "Gen. Norman D. Cota. He said, 'Twenty-nine, let's go,' and off we went." The last thing Sessno did before going off the air was congratulate me for my forty-fifth wedding anniversary. Unbeknownst to me, he had spoken to my daughter Bonnie on the phone and was informed by her.

I would be remiss in failing to mention what happened to me after the CNN interview. I was due back in Vierville for an important ceremony that evening, so Mr. Sessno and CNN reporters Bruce Morton and Joan Woodruff, although very tired from twelve hours of broadcasting, made certain that I arrived in Vierville. Their hotel was in Caen, the opposite direction from Vierville, but they got me there in time. That evening in Vierville, I met an attractive and interesting couple from Marly-le-Roi, France, Ginette and Michel Brouchot, who are still our good friends. Madame Brouchot was wearing a photo of an American GI around her neck. They told me that they had adopted this American soldier's grave, which they decorated with flowers every June 6. The soldier, Sgt. Daniel P. Womack from Lynchburg, Virginia, was killed on D-Day while landing with my outfit, Company B, 116th. I asked the Brouchots how they had come to choose this one soldier. They told me that they had wanted to honor a Catholic boy who had died on D-Day. This loving tribute by these wonderful French people for a dead American made a lasting impression on me. Through Bob Sales, we were able to put them in touch with Sergeant Womack's family in Virginia.

Being in France, especially in Normandy, for the fiftieth anniversary of D-Day was a unique event, and the French people could not have been more gracious. They hosted us at lavish lunches and dinners. Naturally, all the meals included wine, and often calvados (apple whiskey). We visited the St. James Cemetery on June 3, where forty-five hundred of our American heroes are buried. The previous day, local schoolchildren had decorated the graves. During our visit, one child stood behind each of the crosses or Stars of David and at a signal each simultaneously released a dove. Then the veterans marched down the main street of Saint-Lô while holding the hands of the local children. The children gave us hand-painted welcome posters, and we gave them gum, as the GIs had done in World War II. Almost the entire population of the town lined the streets, despite the light rain, to applaud us. They yelled out, "*Merci.*" The walls of the buildings had the words "Welcome to the Liberators" painted on them. When we arrived in a huge parkway in Vire, after a grand parade through the town, we were each formally decorated. The governor of Normandy, Monsieur Rene Garrec, with a kiss on each cheek, pinned us with the Jubilee Normandy Liberation Medal. The Twenty-ninth Division Light Soldiers and band were present. Throughout all these ceremonies, both countries' national anthems were played while their respective flags were raised and saluted.

Hal Baumgarten marching in Saint-Lô with local children. Dr. Edmund Beecham is on the left.

One of the days of the fiftieth anniversary celebration, Boyd Cook, Felix Branham, and I were chosen to present a painting to the city of Saint-Lô. The painting, *The Twenty-ninth Division on Omaha Beach,* was presented at the city hall, Hotel de Ville, to Vice Mayor Jean Mignon.

The crowning event of the fiftieth anniversary was on June 6 in the American cemetery at Colville. Surrounded by U.S. congressmen, cabinet members, Walter Cronkite, chief of staff of the U.S. Army, and other dignitaries, President Clinton addressed us, the VIPs. His speech was very touching and stirring. An air force jet flyover in formation followed the president's speech. After his address, the president shook my hand and even asked me what I had done on D-Day. I told him that I did what he had alluded to in his speech, "That many soldiers, although already wounded, went up the bluff to continue fighting." He then thanked me. Rita and I met Hillary Clinton, who graciously posed for photos with us. At

Hal Baumgarten conversing with First Lady Hillary Clinton at the Colville American cemetery, following D-Day ceremony.

a later date she autographed them. In my conversation with her, she requested a copy of my newly published book. When I returned home, I sent her an autographed copy for the White House library. As the president and Mrs. Clinton were being ushered out by the Secret Service, I was standing three deep in the crowd. President Clinton broke into the crowd, grasped my hand, and said, "Thanks again."

On June 10, along with my fellow Twenty-niners, I marched up the Champs-Élysées in formation. At the Arc de Triomphe, the French army chief of staff, with a handshake and a salute, greeted us. Over a loudspeaker, we could hear the sound of waves coming in on the Normandy beaches. Even though I have neglected to relate all of the magnificent lunches, dinners, and other events, one can see this was an incredible and unforgettable trip.

Hal with his British D-Day veteran comrades in Arromanches during the fifty-fifth anniversary ceremony, June 1999.

Five years later I returned to Normandy for the fifty-fifth anniversary of D-Day. We flew Air France, and the pilot welcomed us on the PA system, saying, "I hope your landing in France will be more pleasant this time." The people of Normandy were as great as they have always been to us.

On June 5, 1999, I was given a front-row seat of honor with British veterans at a ceremony in Arromanches, the British sector on D-Day. The most impressive part of this event was receiving a medallion, a certificate, and a handshake from Monsieur Garrec, the governor of Normandy, and Jacques Chirac, the president of France. Rita and I then visited their fine D-Day museum.

On the morning of June 6, Mayor Oxeant of Vierville requested that I speak at our Twenty-ninth Division monument in the center of the town. That day I gave the following brief address:

Fifty-fifth anniversary of D-Day at the Twenty-ninth Division monument at Vierville-sur-Mer.

Mayor Oxeant, Vierville-sur-Mer, congratulates Hal after his speech in front of the Twenty-ninth Division monument, June 6, 1999.

Mayor Oxeant, distinguished guests, people of Vierville, and fellow Twenty-niners:

As I looked out at the beach from the protection of the sea wall, the beach was strewn with dead 116th Infantry soldiers—like the refuse of a large shipwreck. By the time I started up the bluff toward Vierville, I had already been wounded two times. Thus, I am in much better health standing here in Vierville today. My first return trip to Vierville was in September 1988, when we dedicated this monument to the Twenty-ninth Division. We thank you Monsieur Mayor and the people of Vierville for taking such good care of it. It is wonderful how the new generation of French people keep the memory of D-Day alive.

I feel the presence now of my fellow Twenty-niners, who sacrificed their lives to liberate this city. They would say, as I do today, "it was all worthwhile."

Je vous remercie de votre bonte.

The local French people, ex-underground fighters, my fellow

Twenty-ninth Division members, tourists from the America, and even the mayor of Bedford, Virginia had gathered to hear me talk. It was a great honor. After my short address to the large crowd, the mayor of Bedford congratulated me and presented me with the key to the city of Bedford. This I wear on my Twenty-ninth Division overseas hat along with the Bedford County Seal pin given to me by Lucille Bogess, the sister of Bedford and Raymond Hoback. Fran Sherr Davino, our tour leader and good friend, arranged all of the above-mentioned ceremonies. Fran's father, Mel Sherr, was one of the Twenty-ninth Division heroes on D-Day.

The ceremonies on June 6 continued at Saint-Lô. The mayor, city council, president of the district of La Manche, and wonderful people of Saint-Lô greeted us. They presented us with a fifty-fifth anniversary bronze Saint-Lô medallion and gave us a fantastic banquet. The president of La Manche invited us for a gourmet dinner at the provincial capitol building on another evening. Throughout our entire trip, young uniformed British reenactors accompanied us. These great guys, who were filmed in the battle scenes of *Saving Private Ryan,* wore World War II-type uniforms and insignia. At the Twenty-ninth Division wall at Saint-Jean-de-Savigny, I had a personal plaque dedicated to me. The quotation on my bronze plaque reads, "Never forget my buddies."

We were guests one afternoon at a lavish party hosted by the Count and Countess Kergorlay at their magnificent Chateau de Canisy. They held this party to thank the soldiers for delivering their chateau from its German occupiers during the war. We sampled caviar, smoked salmon, wine, champagne, scotch, and pastries in this opulent palace.

On June 9, we visited the Chapelle de la Madeleine. This museum in Saint-Lô holds flags, artifacts, plaques, and books of World War II, but no weapons. Monsieur Jean

Plaque on Twenty-ninth Division Wall of Remembrance at Saint-Jean-de-Savigny.

Hal with his plaque on the Twenty-ninth Division Wall of Remembrance in Saint-Jean-de-Savigny, surrounded by British reenactors, June 1999.

Count and Countess Kergorlay with their children.

Hal and Rita as guests of the Count and Countess Kergorlay at their chateau, June 1999.

Mignon, my good friend, is the *gardien,* or curator of this museum. My books can be found in a glass case there. That evening, my good friend Dr. Claude Paris and his lovely wife, Odile, entertained a group of us at their home and treated us to dinner at a fine restaurant. Claude is a veterinarian and author who owns a champion hunter, Gloire St. Loise.

In between the commemorative activities on June 6, I found time to walk the beach at Vierville. Along the way I once again met the marvelous Brouchots. They had just come from decorating Daniel Womack's grave with a large bouquet of flowers. Reaching the beach, I saw that signs now designate the boundaries of Dog Green and Charlie sectors. I found my landing area on the western flank of Dog Green sector. Going up the bluff on the right flank, I

Interior of La Chapelle de La Madeleine in Saint-Lô, now a museum, dates to the twelfth century.

was able to come face to face with that huge death-dealing pillbox of D-Day, WN 73. Up close, it is unbelievably huge, with very thick cement walls. The greenery of the bluff covers its northern wall, but its aperture looks east, which gives it a clear field of fire sidewise, over the entire beach below. This pillbox's MG42 fire was devastating to the landing troops. Its protection from naval and air bombardment was obvious.

While in Vierville that day, a Frenchman asked me if I was a D-Day veteran. When I answered in the affirmative, he beckoned me to follow him up the hill to his little truck. This man was wearing full leg boots and carrying a bucket, much like a fisherman. He handed me a white plastic bag, which I thought contained a fish. To my amazement, it held a U.S. Army canteen. This canteen had some caked-on mud

Hal Baumgarten on Omaha Beach, June 6, 1999. Sign denotes boundaries of Charlie and Dog Green sectors.

Ginette and Michel Brouchot with Hal, Vierville-sur-Mer, June 6, 1999.

on its surface but otherwise was in excellent condition. He wanted to know if it was authentic. Then he related to me that it was found that morning in the southwest area of Vierville, the same area I had fought through with my walking wounded on D-Day. It was incredible that a farmer tilling the soil on June 6, 1999, fifty-five years after D-Day, would unearth this canteen. He gave it to me saying, "*Pour vous.*" I thought that it could have been one of the canteens I drank from on D-Day and discarded. It was eerie, but meant to be. I donated it to a museum in Punta Gorda, Florida.

I met Dr. Ambrose in the American cemetery on June 9. I was always in awe of this friend and great American historian. He prodded me to write my books and was kind to write about me in his own books, *D-Day* and *The Victors*. Many other authors have also written about my D-Day experiences. At the time of this book's publication, I have been mentioned in thirty-eight books, besides my own. Dr. Ronald Drez wrote about me in his *Voices of D-Day* and in his more recent *Voices of Valor*. Alexander Kershaw, a great author and screenwriter, wrote *Bedford Boys*. In this book, he mentions me and my close relationship with the Company A Bedford guys. Rev. John Schildt wrote the most complete, excellent history of the Stonewall Brigade, 116th Infantry. His fine book, *The Long Line of Splendor, 1742-1992*, also includes my history. Douglas Keeney and William S. Butler's pictorial, *Days of Destiny*, has a quote from me. Jonathan Gawne, in his terrific book, *Spearheading D-Day*, acknowledges my assistance and information. My Company A buddy John Barnes wrote *Fragments of My Life with Company A, 116th Regiment*. In this book, he tells his readers to read my book to find out about D-Day. One of the most concise pieces of coverage about the invasion of Normandy is *Voices from D-Day*, by Jonathan Bastable. He, too, mentions me.

Thus, the fifty-fifth anniversary of D-Day was another great event for me, but it was dwarfed by the magnitude of the celebration five years earlier. It was also Rita's and my fiftieth wedding anniversary, which made it even more memorable.

XVII

The National World War II Museum

THEY WILL NOT BE FORGOTTEN

It was like a dream come true. The National World War II Museum opened and was dedicated on June 6, 2000, as the National D-Day Museum and has since been designated by Congress as the United States' official World War II museum. The museum was the brainchild of Dr. Stephen E. Ambrose, professor of history at the University of New Orleans. He had noted the relationship between New Orleans and the various D-days, or amphibious invasions, of World War II. Andrew Jackson Higgins had mass-produced thousands of assault boats in that city. These boats, or copies of them, were used to land the marines and soldiers on beaches for all the D-days of World War II. Gen. Dwight Eisenhower told Dr. Ambrose that the Higgins boats won the war. Armed with this knowledge, in the 1980s Ambrose founded the Eisenhower Center at his university and began collecting oral histories from World War II veterans. These oral histories were stored on audiocassette tapes in a couple of small, cramped classrooms in the history building at the University of New Orleans. The Eisenhower Center proceeded to raise funds for a National World War II Museum. I was one of the "charter" contributors.

Since 1990, Dr. Ambrose has written the biographies of Richard Nixon and Dwight Eisenhower. In 1994, for the fiftieth anniversary of D-Day, he used his huge collection of oral histories to write *D-Day: The Climactic Battle of World War II.* This great book serves as a reminder of the sacrifices of veterans to secure peace and freedom. Pres. Bill Clinton used this book for his June 6, 1994, address in the American cemetery at Colville, Normandy, commemorating the fiftieth anniversary of the D-Day invasion. Dr. Ambrose followed up with two other books, *The Victors* and *Citizen Soldier.* A very large chunk of his profits went to the National World War II Museum.

I was very excited about going to New Orleans for the opening of the museum. Dr. Gordon "Nick" Mueller, chairman of the National World War II Museum, sent me two ID tags and invitations to all of the opening events. One of my tags was labeled "D-Day Veteran" and the other stated "Distinguished Guest." Since I have a married daughter, Karen Sher, and two lovely granddaughters, Rose and Samantha, in New Orleans, I arrived a day earlier, on June 2, so that Rita and I could attend Rose's confirmation. Upon arriving at the Fairmont Hotel, a phone call was waiting for me from Ms. Claudia Barker. Ms. Barker requested that I be prepared to speak at the Victory Dinner on June 5. This was an honor that I quickly accepted, although Rita advised me that I would probably be one of many veterans chosen to speak.

On Saturday, June 3, Rita and I were invited to a founder's VIP reception cocktail party and an advance tour of the museum. It didn't take long for me to realize what a great honor it was for me to have been invited to this affair. Besides meeting my good friend Dr. Stephen Ambrose and his lovely wife, Moira, I met Dr. Mueller and his charming wife, Beth, for the first time. The latter were dressed in 1940s-era attire for the USO dance and show that evening. They looked so good, I had to photograph them. Our son-in-law, Leopold Sher, introduced Rita and I to Mayor Marc Morial of New Orleans. We met Steven Forbes, former senator and presidential candidate George McGovern, and Secretary of Defense William Cohen and his beautiful "partner," wife Janet Langhorne. Then I was able to have a one-on-one conversation with the Academy Award-winning actor Tom Hanks, a friendly, down-to-earth person. I told Tom that I thought he deserved an Oscar for *Saving Private Ryan*. My favorite moment of the movie was the stop-action look at Captain Miller's blood-splattered face in the opening combat scene. From the expression on his face, I could

Hal Baumgarten conversing with Tom Hanks at the National World War II Museum, June 5, 2000.

envision all of the horror on the Dog Green sector of the beach. I received a nice letter from him after this meeting. However, with no return address, I couldn't answer it. Meeting Steven Spielberg was a real thrill for me. I can only think of one appropriate Yiddish word that best describes this down-to-earth genius—*mench*. He related that he had borrowed much information from the museum, but parts of the beach combat scenes had came from my museum cassette history. I had suspected this, but to hear it from his lips validated my belief.

After many of the dignitaries had spoken, including some salient remarks from Dr. Ambrose, we were treated to a preview tour of the museum. The Louisiana Memorial Pavilion, the large entrance room of the museum, had a newly built LCVP, or Higgins boat, in its northwest corner. There were various kinds of World War II armored vehicles surrounding the northern and eastern areas of this large room. Hanging from the ceiling at the northeast corner, looking like a toy, was a real World War II British Spitfire fighter plane. As we proceeded toward the ascending staircase, I noticed the floor was covered with inscribed donated bricks. I have two bricks in section nineteen. The Normandy D-Day exhibits were on the third floor. The displays of photos, uniforms, armament, and audiovisual aids were fantastic. There were a few small listening rooms for voice-overs. One room featured my good buddy Bob Slaughter (Company D, 116th) and another, Felix Branham (Company K, 116th).

Our children took us out to dinner that evening at Commander's Palace, one of New Orleans' finest restaurants, so we did not attend the gala USO show and dance at the Fairmont Hotel. However, two of my Twenty-niners, George Cook (Company F, 104th quartermaster) and Sergio Maddelena (Company F, 116th) really enjoyed it.

On Sunday, June 4, I received a phone call from Alvin

Rita with Tom Hanks at the World War II Museum, June 5, 2000.

Rita and Hal Baumgarten with Tom Hanks in the National World War II Museum, June 5, 2000. Note the real World War II British Spitfire fighter plane hanging from the ceiling in background.

Hal Baumgarten conversing with Steven Spielberg in the National World War II Museum, June 5, 2000.

Ungerleider (Company L, 115th), a retired brigadier general and past national commander of the Twenty-ninth Division Association. Al advised me that some media people were doing a documentary and were seeking World War II D-Day veterans of German and Austrian Jewish extraction. The interviews were going to be used either for foreign television or the Discovery Channel. While they were interviewing us, Dr. Ambrose, who had been advised that I was in that particular hotel lounge room, entered the room and was filmed greeting us.

On Monday, June 5, I went to the huge ballroom at the Hilton Hotel to hear panelists speak. Dr. Stephen Ambrose, Ronald Drez, author of *Voices of D-Day* and *Voices of Valor*, and others spoke about the D-Day landings. We Twenty-niners sat together in VIP seats. Beside me, there were John

Robertson (Company F, 116th), Sergio Maddelena, George Cook (Company F, 104th quartermaster), and Gen. Robert Ploger (121st engineer). John Slaughter (Company D, 116th) was on the first panel. Even though we all knew John's D-Day story, we enjoyed hearing him say that all Twenty-niners have a close comradeship, "like brothers." I had to leave early to get dressed for the formal Victory Dinner and missed Steven Spielberg's showing of his "Combat Cameraman" preview film.

With my prepared talk in my tuxedo pocket, I went with Rita to the museum for a cocktail party. Once again, we mingled with dignitaries: seven Congressional Medal of Honor winners, ministers of defense of seven NATO countries, Senators John Breaux and Mary Landrieu of Louisiana, Mayor Morial, Secretary of Transportation Slayton, Secretary of Defense Cohen, Dr. Stephen Ambrose, and Dr. Gordon Mueller. This was a very push party. Of course, my friendly chatter continued with Tom Hanks and Steven Spielberg. We took many photos. Some brief speeches were made, and I was expecting to be called up to talk. As the party wound down, I began to wonder if they had decided not to use me as a speaker.

At about 9:00 P.M., we were bused to the Fairmont Hotel for the Victory Dinner. Sitting next to me on the bus were Rep. William Jefferson and Sen. John Breaux, both of Louisiana. On my way to the Fairmont's ballroom, I passed Dr. Mueller, who was walking in the opposite direction. He said, "Got your speech ready, Hal?" I answered in the affirmative and offered him a typed intro to use. He waved it off, saying, "I know more about you than you think." It was a relief to know that I was really going to be a speaker, but I was surprised to find out that I was the only veteran who was scheduled to speak, especially since there were seven Congressional Medal of Honor holders at the dinner. We were seated at the front table. The dinner had five hundred large museum contributors present. At our table was the minister of defense of Luxembourg, a very interesting personality. Also present at our table was the granddaughter of Private Nyland, the man represented in the movie *Saving Private Ryan*. My daughter Karen and her husband, Lee Sher, were also seated with us.

This Victory Dinner was to honor the benefactors of the National World War II Museum. I was certainly going to thank them in my talk for making this magnificent museum a reality. Looking around, I saw, along with many of the celebrities I had already recognized, Miss America, Heather French, at an adjacent table. While we were being served gourmet food and fine wines, the speakers commenced. The mayor of New Orleans was first, followed by Gov. Mike Foster of Louisiana, the secretary of Commerce, Secretary of Defense Cohen, and Miss America.

Just when my delicious-looking filet mignon was served, Dr. Mueller introduced me. He announced that the next speaker had landed with the first wave on D-Day, wearing a special jacket. He mentioned that my field jacket had a Star of David painted on it. As I ascended the speaker's platform, I had to think of a quick ad lib. Dr. Mueller had, unknowingly, preempted what I was going to say about my jacket. Thus, when I spoke, I said, "Yes, I was wearing a special jacket on D-Day to let Hitler know who I was." I received a standing ovation for that remark. In my address I mentioned some of my D-Day buddies by name and how they had died. Many in the audience had tears in their eyes. I related to them how important the D-Day story was to my fellow D-Day veterans and me, especially to honor those true heroes of D-Day who paid the supreme sacrifice. These wonderful people have insured that the D-Day story would be permanently perpetuated by the National World War II Museum. I thanked them and Dr. Stephen E. Ambrose, "the greatest American historian of the twentieth century," from the bottom of my heart. As I descended from the speaker's platform to the sound of thundering applause, Dr. Ambrose was the first one to congratulate me, with a bear hug.

Following me on the dais was Tom Hanks. In good humor, he ad-libbed, "Sure, they had me follow the veteran . . . a tough act to follow. He is the real thing, and I am just an actor." About midnight, after talks by Steven Spielberg, Tom Brokaw, and Dr. Ambrose, the dinner was over. I found it interesting that Tom Brokaw quoted me by calling Dr. Ambrose the "greatest American historian of the twentieth century." As Secretary Cohen shook my hand, he said, "You brought tears to my eyes." Mr. Forbes and Steven Spielberg both congratulated me. It was a tremendously humbling occasion.

We didn't achieve much sleep that evening, because Rita and I were invited for the official opening ceremony early the next morning. They served us a continental breakfast in an air-conditioned tent adjacent to the museum. The official ribbon cutting and dedication ceremony were going to take place about 8:00 A.M. The same array of illustrious dignitaries were seated in front of the museum for the ceremony, minus Governor Foster, who had to be in the state capital. Rita and I had front-row reviewing stand seats. For a brief time a few sprinkles dampened the multitude of spectators, and I thought to myself that perhaps it was God's way of shedding some tears of joy. One of the speakers, Secretary of Transportation Slayton, mentioned my talk from the previous evening. Two of my Twenty-niners were present, Bob Slaughter and Charles Neighbors (Company E, 116th).

Following the ribbon cutting that officially opened the National World War II Museum on June 6, 2000, the largest parade since World War II passed by the reviewing stands. All the present D-Day veterans and their respective outfits were represented. There were squadrons of airplane fly-overs, with at least fifty airplanes of all types. Two of the trucks in the parade had Twenty-ninth Division banners on them; however, only the second truck had Twenty-niners on-board. I recognized George Cook, Doyle Chambers (Second Battalion, 175th), Gen. Robert Ploger, Tom Johnson, John Robertson, Alvin Ungerleider, and Donald Van Roosen, commander-elect of the Twenty-ninth Division Association. Incidentally, the front page of the next day's *New Orleans Times-Picayune* pictured the Twenty-ninth Division truck with the confetti streaming down over it. Some of the faces in the picture were concealed by the tons of falling red, white, and blue confetti. While reviewing the parade, I was interviewed by the local NBC affiliate and U.S. Armed Forces Television.

After the parade, Rita and I were taken by bus to the New Orleans Arena, where a three-hour grand show took place. It commenced with four beautifully costumed girls who sang World War II songs and danced. Miss America sang the national anthem. There were British and French service bands, Eighty-second Airborne group singers, U.S. Marine and Navy bands, a soldier singing about "never forgetting," and a children's singing group. The latter group culminated with "God Bless America," with audience participation. There were speeches delivered from the stage, with Tom Brokaw acting as the master of ceremonies. Especially stirring was a dramatic recitation by Tom Hanks, who quoted Ernie Pyle's description of the death and destruction seen after the D-Day landings on Omaha Beach. During the celebration festivities, Dr. Ambrose was presented with two honors, a gold U.S. government medal and a doctorate from the University of New Orleans.

Steven Spielberg and Tom Hanks being interviewed by Tom Brokaw, June 6, 2000.

My son, Hal, back in Jacksonville, was watching Tom Brokaw on NBC's *Today Show*. Mr. Brokaw did an early-morning interview with Dr. Ambrose from the museum. Hal became very excited when he heard Dr. Ambrose say, "Hal Baumgarten is a friend of mine. His story of D-Day is one of the most amazing stories." He went on to mention my five wounds in combat and my becoming a physician. My son e-mailed me immediately about the program.

Thus, the fifty-sixth anniversary of D-Day and the opening of the museum were very memorable. The icing on the cake was that Rita and I had celebrated our fifty-first wedding anniversary on June 4. A statement made by Dr. Ambrose made a lasting impression on me. Paraphrasing his words, I recall that he said that during the Second World War, the United States had sent the best of its young people halfway around the world in all directions—not to oppress, not to pillage, not to rape or burn—but to liberate.

XVIII

National D-Day Memorial

REMEMBERING THE BEDFORD BOYS

The Twenty-ninth Division Association changed its annual reunion in 2001, so that it would coincide with the dedication and opening of the National D-Day Memorial at Bedford, Virginia. We were headquartered at a hotel in Roanoke, Virginia, for the dedication, scheduled for June 6, 2001. On June 5, Rita and I drove to Bedford. It is a charming little town in southwest Virginia's Bedford County. If you step too hard on your accelerator, you are out of town. We visited the Bedford Boys monument, on the lawn of the county courthouse. As I looked at those heroes' names on the plaque, I could picture their faces as they had been in 1944.

On June 6, about four hundred Twenty-niners, including family members, boarded buses for the trip to the National D-Day Memorial. We drove along the 116th Infantry Regiment Memorial Highway into the assembly area at the base of the memorial. The National D-Day Memorial, which I wholeheartedly recommend visiting, is an outdoor monument that covers nine acres.

Three hundred sixty tons of green granite were brought in from the national forests of Minnesota to build this magnificent edifice. On ascending the hill from the assembly parking area with George Cook, we viewed the Overlord Arch entranceway. This forty-four-foot, six-inch-high black granite and marble arch is built to that size to denote June 6, '44. Its top is inscribed "Overlord," the name of the Allied D-Day operation. Five points of inlaid granite, representing the five Normandy beaches, alternate in color. Three white marble stripes and two black ones symbolize the stripes painted on Allied planes to protect them from friendly fire on D-Day. Looking through this arch provides a view of the pictur-esque Peaks of Otter of the Blue Ridge Mountains in the distance. On the other side of this beautiful symbolic

The Overlord Arch at the National D-Day Memorial.

arch is a sculptured symbol of the fallen, called *The Final Tribute.* This inverted rifle, stuck in the ground by its bayonet, topped with a helmet and dog tags, is a powerful representation of the graves of the nineteen Bedford Boys who died in the first fifteen minutes of D-Day on Dog Green sector of Omaha Beach. Flags of the twelve Allied nations, which supplied forces and material aid for the landing, ring the perimeter of the memorial.

There are two other sections of the memorial, but we only had time to explore one, so we decided not to visit the English garden, in the form of a patch of the Supreme Headquarters Allied Expeditionary Force, the SHAEF. Our main attention was focused on the middle plaza area, which represents the D-Day invasion. The middle plaza was the most meaningful to me. It features a reflecting pool with a beach. In the middle of the pool, a fountain sprinkles water, giving the pool the appearance of bullets piercing the waves on D-Day. A sculptured assault boat perches at one end, with its ramp down. In the pool life-size bronze soldiers, sculptured by Jim Brothers, seem to struggle ashore. In the water, one bronze soldier wades with his rifle above his head, while another drags a buddy onto the beach. At the beach end is a sculptured cliff, with Rangers ascending it.

With the images of the middle plaza sparking my memories of that day fifty-seven years earlier, I returned to the upper plaza and its Overlord Arch, where the dedication was to take place. George and I were wearing our D-Day veteran badges, but we still had a difficult time getting through the metal detectors and the crowd. I don't believe the D-Day Memorial organizers were prepared for the thousands who came for the dedication. The Brouchots, having traveled all the way from Paris, were locked outside. There were not

The National D-Day Memorial and its life-size bronze soldiers, May 29, 2000.

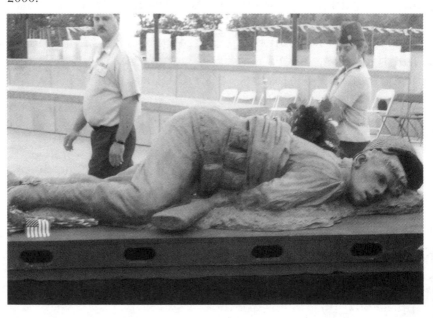

enough seats, and there was no special section to honor the D-Day veterans, so many of the Twenty-niners and their wives had to sit on the ground. Though the D-Day Memorial Foundation Organizing Committee had no control over the weather, the oppressive heat that day also handicapped the event.

I say that God saved me on D-Day to be the spokesman for the true heroes of D-Day. The spirits of the Bedford Boys were in the middle plaza that day. I felt their presence, and though I was not asked to speak, believe that they would have wanted me to talk about their bravery on Dog Green sector. Pres. George W. Bush did mention Bedford Hoback in his speech; however, the plaza was so massive that the president and other speakers could only be seen with binoculars. When they asked all D-Day veterans to stand up and be honored, the entire audience stood.

XIX

USO Trip to Bosnia

MORALE BUILDING

At the Twenty-ninth Division annual reunion at Ocean City, Maryland, in October 2000, Gen. H. Steven Blum was the keynote speaker. He told us that he would like to take some of the D-Day veterans to Bosnia in 2001. At our next Twenty-ninth Division meeting in June 2001, for the opening of the D-Day Memorial, General Blum invited me to go to Bosnia for Thanksgiving. I told him he would have to ask Rita. When he did, Rita questioned, "Who is going to protect my husband?" The general told her that he would personally guard me (and he did).

Maj. Drew Sullins, General Blum's aide, made all the arrangements with the USO. No one can refuse General Blum. Thus, with the sponsorship of our great USO, ten Twenty-niners embarked for Bosnia on November 18, 2001. Our trip was billed as "Spend a Holiday with Heroes." Dr. Stephen E. Ambrose and his lovely wife, Moira, led our group, which also included Art Van Cook from the 111th, Austin Cox, Dana Tawes, Alvin Ungerleider, and Jack Wetstine from the 115th, Bob Slaughter and Donald

McCarthy from the 116th, and Donald Van Roosen, and Joe Farinholt from the 175th, all D-Day veterans.

We traveled to Sarajevo, Bosnia, via Vienna on Austrian Airlines. When we arrived in Sarajevo, it was snowing. From the airport we had to travel in a van northeast around the mountains to get to Eagle Base at Tuzla. None of us had any idea of the impact our visit was going to have on the servicemen at the various bases in Bosnia. How could ten old battle veterans and Dr. and Mrs. Ambrose have any affect on these young warriors of the twenty-first century? Upon arriving at the base after our three-hour trip in the snow, we found out immediately. General Blum and his men saluted, greeted us warmly, shook our hands, and told us how honored they were to have us.

We soon found out that base life had changed significantly

Dr. Stephen Ambrose (my hero) giving a victory sign before we boarded our Black Hawk helicopter at Eagle Base.

Dr. Ambrose and Major Sullins at Eagle Base, November 2001.

since our own service in the military. At the Longhorn Mess Hall, one of the two great eating-places of Eagle Base, we received our first super meal. No longer was there a KP for the troops. The Longhorn was open twenty-four hours a day, with local Bosnians serving anything you could want to eat or drink, except alcohol. They were very strict about possession of alcohol on the base. They had yellow amnesty boxes in which the soldiers could get rid of any booze without punishment. While we were enjoying dinner at the Longhorn, where they even supplied the calorie content of the foods, General Blum sat next to me, eating an ice-cream cone. He said to me, "I'm going to fatten you up, Hal." After dinner we were taken to the Audie Murphy Inn, where we were housed two to a room. I chose Don McCarthy as my roommate; I knew he didn't snore.

Our schedule was very busy. Our first day began with breakfast at the Longhorn, where I had an egg-white omelet. Then we visited Comanche Base by way of two Black Hawk helicopters, which were armed. This was the base of "Task Force Sword," an attack group. We were able to examine the attack helicopters and were presented with personal certificates of excellence. Here I met Neal Edmunds from Ponte Vedra Beach, Florida, my home area. I took his picture with his attack helicopter and sent it to his father, retired major general Maurice Edmonds, when I returned home.

Returning to Eagle Base, we had the opportunity to examine the huge Abrams tank, which guarded the base's entrance. I enjoyed attending the firearms training simulator, and I was able to fire the M-16 rifle, 9 mm pistol, and machine gun. The range was completely electronic, and I qualified "expert" with the M-16 and 9 mm pistol. Frankly, I would prefer my old M-1 in combat.

After dinner, the entire base was brightly lit. We heard the "Beer Barrel Polka" blaring over loudspeakers. I didn't know that this song was that of the Twenty-ninth Division. We were invited to the beautiful headquarters building with its "Twenty-ninth Division fountain." In its auditorium, Major Sullins projected each of our World War II photos on a large screen. He told the audience of officers about our World War II actions. Next, General Blum personally presented each of us with the Task Force Eagle Medallion.

The next day, we flew to Conner Base and met the soldiers. Our Black Hawk helicopter was armed with rockets and machine guns. On our approach, we flew over the Drena River, where Serbs had thrown the bodies of raped and murdered Muslims. Landing in Srebrenica, we were guarded by armored cars. This was a war area, the city where Serbs had brutally clubbed to death thousands of Muslims.

Every day troops uncovered arms caches, including shoulder-to-air missiles. Nearby was a mass grave where twelve hundred Muslims were buried. In Bosnia, the U.S. Army was protecting Muslims from such ethnic cleansing.

That evening, General Blum and his staff feted us at a formal dinner at the Balkan Grille. He brought some soldiers into the dining room and told them that we Twenty-niners had set very high standards. It was his hope that they would try to follow in our footsteps. Our coffee mugs had the Twenty-ninth Division insignia on them, and we were encouraged by General Blum to keep them. I did and still treasure my cup.

The next day was Thanksgiving. Dr. Ambrose and my comrades returned to Comanche Base for a book signing. I went with Major Sullins to the Eagle Base hospital to speak to the medical staff about World War II medicine. Most of the people walking into the room seemed to come in reluctantly; however, once I started speaking about D-Day on Dog Green sector, they could not hear enough. After speaking and answering questions, ninety minutes had elapsed. Afterward, a small ceremony was held in which I was presented with the Task Force Medical Eagle Medallion by the commanding officer. There was a blue and gray Twenty-ninth Division insignia on one side of it.

That day was busy. We met the touring general Richard Myers, chief of the general staff of the United States. We dedicated the base's fitness center in honor of Frank Peregory. Frank was a member of Company K, 116th, who was considered the "Sergeant York of World War II." He was our first Congressional Medal of Honor winner. Then we had a service in the base chapel for our fallen comrades. I was shocked when Sergeant Rappaport was called to the front of the chapel and proceeded to say the Hebrew *Kadish,* the remembrance prayer for the dead. This was probably because General Blum is Jewish. The next activity of the day was to rededicate Salute Alley as Twenty-ninth Division Way.

That evening we had a wonderful Thanksgiving feast with the soldiers in the Balkan Grille. These fine men asked me if they could sit with us. They brought me my pumpkin pie desert, not allowing me to get up in order to serve myself. Their appetites were not only for the delicious food and magnificent desserts, but also for information about D-Day.

After dinner, we autographed Dr. Ambrose's books on D-Day in the post exchange, known as the PX. At about 7:30 P.M., we were seated on an auditorium stage as a panel. The crowd was so large that some had to stand. We answered the innumerable questions of the soldiers of Eagle Base. What a fine group of young men, all volunteers.

On our final day at Eagle Base, we had a sumptuous breakfast. After good-byes from General Blum and his staff, we got into a luxury bus. It was going to be a three-hour ride to Sarajevo in a snowstorm. This bus was stocked with food, fruit, soft drinks, and bottled water. It had a number of full-sized beds and two living rooms. The bus ride was very enjoyable for me, because I had the opportunity to discuss history with my great friend, Dr. Stephen Ambrose.

Once in Sarajevo, we were able to visit the PXs at the huge Burit Army Base. Then our group had lunch at its Burger King. In Sarajevo, we were housed in a Holiday Inn that had been bombed by the Serbs. Austin Cox and I found out how inexpensive it was to have a couple of scotches at the local bar, then we had dinner of beer and pizza at an Italian restaurant. The next morning, with snow falling, we visited and took a group photo at the bridge where Archduke Ferdinand had been assassinated. This event had started World War I.

Next we flew to Vienna and were housed at the Hilton on

Posing on bridge where Archduke Ferdinand was assassinated, Sarajevo, Bosnia, November 2001. Top row, left to right: Farinholt, Steve Ambrose, Moira, Slaughter, Tawes, Ungerleider, Van Cook, Wetstine. Lower row, left to right: McCarthy, Sullins, Hal, Austin-Cox.

Moira and Steve Ambrose in Sarajevo, November 2001.

the Danube. Our rooms were wonderful. That evening, we went to Kronprinz Rudolf Saal Heurigenausschank for an Austrian dinner, drinks, and entertainment. Dinner was followed by a visit to a coffee house, Café Cobenzl, for champagne and coffee. From there we could see the entire city of Vienna, with its beautiful evening lights.

The next morning, we were off for the U.S. Midway over the Atlantic Ocean, a call came over the airplane's PA system, requesting a physician. I volunteered to treat a Georgia man, who was having a heart attack. While treating him, a familiar face peered out from a curtain in first class. It was Steve Ambrose, trying to see what was going on. We had an old standard joke between us. My father had wanted me to become a teacher, and his father had wished that he would become a doctor. I said to him, "You see why I should have been a history teacher, instead of a physician?" When we arrived at Dulles Airport, I had a live patient.

I will never forget this special trip, meeting the soldiers, and the comradeship of my fellow Twenty-niners. Also, I had the great pleasure of being with Moira and Dr. Stephen E. Ambrose as well as Gen. H. Steven Blum, two of my personal heroes.

XX

Opening of the Pacific Wing

NATIONAL WORLD WAR II MUSEUM

On our trip to Bosnia, Dr. Ambrose asked me to be present for the opening of the Pacific wing of the National World War II Museum on December 7, 2001. Of course, Rita and I attended. At the membership preview on December 5, he told a large group of Pacific veterans, "I have a Normandy D-Day veteran present. I will introduce him later." I immediately handed my camera to Rita, because I thought he was going to call on me to speak. Instead, he said some flattering things about me, and then said, "Hal, come up to the front of the room and turn around so everybody can see you."

On December 7, 2001, the sixtieth anniversary of the surprise attack on Pearl Harbor, the Pacific wing of the National World War II Museum opened. The celebration of this event was, as usual, organized with the creativeness that only the National World War II Museum, with Dr. Stephen E. Ambrose as founder and Dr. Gordon Mueller as CEO, and the city of New Orleans are capable of carrying out. While the city's church bells pealed, words were spoken by distinguished guests, among them former president George H. Bush, Tom Hanks, Louisiana lieutenant governor Kathleen Blanco, and Texas governor Rick Perry. These speakers were followed with a flyover by B-17s and B-24s, a victory parade of army, navy, coast guard, and marine bands, and World War II Pacific veterans. This celebration took place in the presence of twelve Congressional Medal of Honor recipients, who further honored the proceedings.

During the week, there was a reenactment landing on Lake Pontchartrain Beach, a USO dance and dinner, and a gala black tie banquet. Preceded by a special Pacific documentary film premiere at the Orpheum Theatre, the gala banquet was a lavish formal affair held the evening of the seventh at the Marriott Hotel. At the banquet, Dr. Ambrose, displaying his sense of humor, wore his "Meriwether Lewis costume," a white shirt with fancy lace collar and sleeves, bright red jacket with gold buttons, black knickers, and red long stockings. The next evening, December 8, we were invited to the Congressional Medal of Honor Winner's Banquet at Harrah's Casino. As I looked around, I realized I was the only veteran not wearing the coveted medal.

The next day, we were invited to an academic symposium at the exclusive Plimsol Club, on the top floor of the World Trade Center building. The title of the talks was "Pacific Peace: U.S.-Japanese Diplomacy 1945-Present." The keynote speaker was Ambassador Richard C. Holbrooke. The Japanese ambassador and Dr. Ambrose also spoke. A heroic veteran of World War II was present, George Tenney. George was a POW in the Pacific from 1941 through 1945 and had lived through torture and slave labor in the coal mines. During the ordeal, he lost ninety pounds. What bothered George the most was that "the Japanese never said they were sorry."

Hal with Steve Ambrose in his Meriwether Lewis costume at National World War II Museum's Pacific wing opening ball, December 7, 2001.

Moira and Steve Ambrose.

Left to right: Dr. Gordon Mueller, Dr. Stephen Ambrose, and Harold Baumgarten at the Congressional Medal of Honor Winners' Banquet celebrating the opening of the Pacific wing of the National World War II Museum, December 6, 2001.

Rita and Hal in the World War II Museum, December 6, 2001.

Hal with Dr. Stephen Ambrose at the Pacific opening of the National World War II Museum, December 7, 2001.

The events commemorating the opening of the Pacific wing were enjoyable life experiences. I realized, by the fact that we were invited to all the many affairs of the week, what a good friend Dr. Ambrose was to us

XXI

Death of Dr. Stephen E. Ambrose

A TRAGEDY FOR THE WORLD

October 13, 2002, Dr. Stephen E. Ambrose died of his battle with lung cancer. This was a very sad day for Rita and I. I had lost my beloved mother from lung cancer, and Dr. Ambrose's death was another harsh reminder of the pain that disease causes. I was honored to be called to speak at a memorial service for him on October 19. The service was to be held at the front of the National World War II Museum. I accepted with a heavy, mournful heart. The only air travel Rita and I could arrange arrived at noon on the nineteenth, so we had to fly dressed for the occasion. Fortunately, my daughter Karen picked us up at the New Orleans terminal. We arrived at the museum in time for lunch and met some of the other participants, Tom Brokaw, former president George H. Bush, former senator George McGovern, and Lindy Boggs, former congresswoman of Louisiana and the ambassador to the Vatican. There was one other D-Day veteran speaker, Len Lomell.

Dr. Gordon Mueller advised me that some of the speakers were going to be "long winded," so I should please limit my talk. His prediction turned out to be correct, and I eliminated 90 percent of my prepared speech. My introduction was as a colleague, author, and World War II veteran. When I stood at the lectern on the dais, I noted that Moira and the Ambrose family were in the front row. I mentioned my trip to Bosnia with the Ambroses in November 2001 and how Dr. Ambrose had prodded me to write my books. At the conclusion of my short talk, I said that he was not only my good friend, but my hero and idol. His death was a tremendous loss for the entire world. He was only sixty-six years old, and he had many books left in him. Moira and Steve had visited Iwo Jima in 2001 in order to research a book on that battle. *To America*, his final book, was a wonderful review of American history. It was written in the typical, readable Ambrose style.

Hal speaking at Dr. Stephen Ambrose's memorial service in front of the National World War II Museum, October 19, 2002.

His students who spoke painted another picture of Ambrose the teacher. He was said to have once had long hair, and it was rumored that his dog carried his class notes in its mouth. The students said they fought to enroll in his overcrowded classes. Many of them claimed that he had encouraged them to write books.

The entire memorial service was filmed by C-Span. It was attended by thousands of people, including many heartsick veterans. Service color guards and bands were present. Overlooking the service was a huge painting of Dr. Ambrose in the window of the museum. After the memorials were concluded we attended a private cocktail party in the museum. Here we were able to offer our heartfelt condolences to Moira and the Ambrose family members.

The following day my daughter Karen drove us to Dr. Ambrose's Waveland, Mississippi, burial site. It was a shock to see this tiny cemetery by the railroad tracks, where he was buried. The grave was freshly dug, with no headstone. I prayed and shed some tears. I was depressed for weeks after his death. This was the same low feeling I had felt when I lost Cecil Breeden and my D-Day buddies.

XXII

Speaking Engagements 2002-2003

D-DAY MUST NOT BE FORGOTTEN

During the years of 2002 and 2003, I spoke to thousands of people about D-Day. I feel that one of the reasons God saved me on D-Day was to be the spokesman for those who could no longer speak. As of this publication, I am mentioned in forty books about D-Day. My hero buddies will never be recorded in books other than mine. When I speak, I always refer to them by their names and their hometowns.

I have spoken to business clubs, Rotary Clubs, a Meninaks club, churches (including my own synagogue), libraries, dinner clubs, schools, police departments, and even on various cruise ships in South America, France, and the Caribbean.

In January 2002, officer Mike Odle of the Los Angeles Police Department SWAT Team contacted me and requested that I speak at their annual banquet in March. I was flown to Los Angeles and picked up from the airport by Officers Odle and Ryan. After a restful day at a beautiful hotel, I was driven to their banquet. During their cocktail hour, I sold and autographed a small amount of my books.

I found out, after talking to some of their three hundred members, that they operate like an army infantry outfit. They wear helmets, flak jackets, and have military weapons. Some of their training includes daily calisthenics and even jumping out of helicopters.

They were very interested in the D-Day combat as well as the weapons that were used. After I spoke for approximately forty minutes and answered numerous questions, the Los Angeles chief of police thanked me. Then the police department presented me with their official hat and a personalized SWAT Team jacket. I thanked them; however, I expressed privately that it would not get much use in Florida. I was wrong, because in our recent cold waves, the jacket has come in handy.

I had two other March speaking engagements. On March 12, 2002, I spoke to the Rotary Club at the Selva Marina Country Club of Atlantic Beach, Florida. They were a great audience. On March 20, 2002, I spoke at the St. Johns Dinner Club. At the time, I was a member of their board of directors. This was where I found out that women seem to have a greater interest in D-Day than the men. During the question and answer session, the women's questions were more numerous and meaningful than their male counterparts. Perhaps the women were thinking about their own beloved children in similar situations.

On May 1, 2002, I spoke to a standing-room-only crowd at the Neptune Beach, Florida, library. I met some lovely people there. It was a pleasure to meet Lt. David Coffman and J. R. Ross of the Jacksonville Police Department. They have become treasured friends. Subsequently, I spoke on three separate occasions at the Jacksonville Police Academy. I especially stressed in my talks to them leadership, training, and discipline, explaining that despite the cold and seasickness suffered by the men in the D-Day assault boats, those true patriots fought and gave all they had for their fellow soldiers.

In June, I spoke to both of our Southside Business Men's Clubs of Jacksonville. Also in June, I was invited to speak to a group of my peers. I spoke to the D-Day veterans at Alachua, Florida, at the Rebel House Restaurant. Glyn Markham, who owned the restaurant, served on the destroyer *McCook*. This was the ship that blew away the snipers who were intent on killing me on June 7, 1944. Glyn had my book and pictures all over the reception room. This was a moving experience.

I also spoke in nearby Gainesville, Florida, to a large group of Rotarians. During my speech, I mentioned that I had had the greatest plastic surgeon in the world, Dr. Michael Lewin. One of the men buying my book after my talk told me that Dr. Lewin had been his personal friend. He advised me that Dr. Lewin was a Hungarian refugee who had died six months earlier.

On August 20, 2002, I spoke on the *Grand Princess* cruise ship to a group of interested passengers.

Of course, on October 19, 2002, I spoke at Dr. Ambrose's memorial service.

October 30, 2002, I accompanied George Cook and John Hornberger (Company E, 116th) to Fort Benning, Georgia. We met General Long, commanding officer of the Twenty-ninth Division Light and a contingent of our Twenty-niners. After spending a pleasant evening in great accommodations, we helped dedicate a monument to the Twenty-ninth Division. Adjacent to the First Infantry Division Monument, our monument was a wonderful tribute to the Twenty-ninth Infantry Division. Both monuments are on the grounds of the National Infantry Museum at Fort Benning. We had a great weekend of reminiscing and comradeship.

On December 7, 2002, I was the keynote speaker at the

annual banquet of Abota, a prestigious trial lawyer association. The formal dinner was held at the Lodge in Ponte Vedra Beach, Florida. I spoke for about forty minutes to this very interested group. At the end of my talk, Evan Yegelwel, their president, presented me with a check for five hundred dollars for the National World War II Museum. One of my friends in the group, Rutledge Liles, stood up and said that he would match it. Thus, I had one thousand dollars for the museum, to which I added five hundred dollars of my own.

I began the new year's speaking engagements on January 24, 2003, in Punta Gorda, Florida. This was a special event for me, because I was the keynote speaker at the annual reunion of Florida's West Post #2 of the Twenty-ninth Division Association. These were my peers. It was a particular honor to speak to my fellow Twenty-niners. After my talk, they presented me with a large wooden plaque with gold trim and a Twenty-ninth Division insignia. There was a brass plate on it, with the following inscription:

> Presented to Dr. Harold "Hal" Baumgarten A & B Company, 116th Infantry Regiment, and survivor of the first assault wave at Omaha Beach. God has a plan for everybody. You survived those five wounds received on June 6, 1944, to tell the story of liberation for those who remained forever young on that bloody beach. Through your book and your tireless speaking engagements you have preserved a first hand account of history for thousands and, in so doing, you have brought Honor and Glory to the 29th Infantry Division.
>
> His fellow comrades in the 29th Division Association and Florida West Post #2 thank him for a job well done.

I was very touched by this tribute. Joe Joseph, Company B, 116th, made the presentation.

My next important speaking engagement was on June 6, 2003. I spoke in the Louisiana Memorial Pavilion of the National World War II Museum to about four hundred visitors. My wife, Rita, daughter Karen, and her husband, Lee Sher, were in the audience. Though I was told by event organizers that the museum's audiences usually listen for a few minutes and then leave, this large audience, a standing-room-only crowd, stayed throughout my entire talk and the subsequent question and answer session. By the interesting questions I received after my talk, I realized how interested in D-Day the people were. That evening, we attended a lavish victory ball at the Marriott Hotel. I was asked to stand and be recognized. Gen. Norman Schwarzkopf was the guest of honor, and he presented the premiere American

Hal Baumgarten speaking at the National World War II Museum, June 6, 2003.

Moira Ambrose with Hal at the World War II Museum's Victory Ball, June 6, 2003.

Spirit Award of the National World War II Museum to Moira Ambrose, posthumously for Dr. Stephen E. Ambrose. Rita and I enjoyed the evening with our New Orleans children and the Ambrose family members.

During the days of July 19-22, 2003, I was honored to be invited to attend the dedication of the Robert J. Dole Institute of Politics in Lawrence, Kansas. I was to be a guest speaker at what was billed as the "Ultimate World War II Reunion." Rita and I flew to Kansas City, Missouri, where two young soldiers met us; they were holding a sign with my name on it. The soldiers picked up our baggage and placed it in a van for the ride to Lawrence. One soldier was to be our driver 24/7, and the other our escort. When we arrived at our hotel, adjacent to the campus of the University of Kansas, there was a huge banner hanging over the lobby. It stated, "The Greatest Generations' Greatest Celebration." All of our expenses were covered, and we were wined and dined. The other veterans invited were a "who's who" of veterans of World War II. I felt humbled and was very impressed to have been included in the company of such eminent companions as Comanche Navaho Code Talkers, Tuskegee Airmen, Doolittle Raiders, my good friends Walter Ehlers, a Congressional Medal of Honor recipient, and Len Lomell, a Distinguished Service Cross recipient. Walter, Len, and I were some of the veterans on a Normandy panel that took place in the Memory Tent, which held thousands of people. Martin Morgan, research historian of the National World War II Museum, was our moderator. Martin is a good friend and the author of *Down to Earth.*

For lunch on July 21, we were taken to the Circle S Ranch.

Two soldiers picking up Rita and me at the Kansas City, Missouri, airport.

Hal at the Memory Tent, waiting to speak.

Bob Dole met Rita and I at the door. He said, "You came all the way from Florida. I have to get a picture with you." In the dining room, Sen. Elizabeth Dole (North Carolina) was at an adjacent table. She is a gorgeous, delightful person.

That evening we attended a program at the Lied Center of Kansas called "Salute to the Heroes, an Evening to Remember." There was entertainment as well as speakers: Rudy Guilliani, Tom Brokaw, George McGovern, and Bob Dole. The show was a "USO style show and star-studded salute to Bob Dole and all the men and women on the battlefront and home front who rescued civilization in the darkest hour." A humorous part of the show was when a quartet serenaded Bob Dole with "It Had to Be You." The quartet members playfully pawed at Dole's suit and mussed his hair during the number.

Rita and Hal with Bob Dole at the Circle S Ranch in Kansas for lunch, July 19, 2003.

Hal and Rita at lunch with Sen. Elizabeth Dole at the Circle S Ranch, July 19, 2003.

On July 22, we were seated outside for the official dedication ceremony of the Dole Institute of Politics, which was a combined celebration of Mr. Dole's eightieth birthday. Some of the speakers at the dedication were former president Jimmy Carter, Mayor Rudy Guilliani, Tom Brokaw, Kansas governor Kathleen Sebelius, George McGovern, and Condoleezza Rice, the national security advisor. It was marvelous. After the speeches, we toured the Dole Institute. It was a magnificent building that boasts the world's largest stained glass American flag, which was reflected on the building's floor. A "memory wall" was featured on one wall of the institute with 962 8x10-inch photographs. My own World War II photo is on that wall. This whole weekend was outstanding and made me wish that Robert Dole had become our president.

On August 9, we were invited by Lt. Gen. H. Steven Blum, chief of the National Guard Bureau, to attend an officer graduation ceremony at Camp Blanding, Florida. When we arrived at Camp Blanding, we were treated royally. We noted that we had seats with our names at the front of the auditorium. An officer ushered us into a reception room where Maj. Gen. Douglas Burnett of the Florida National Guard and his staff greeted us. After a short while, I heard "Attention!" In walked Lieutenant General Blum and Maj. Drew Sullins. I received a friendly greeting and salute from General Blum. There was an "impromptu ceremony," during which he presented me with his Medallion of Excellence, his three-star red flag decorating one side of it. During his graduation address, General Blum asked me to stand and used my Normandy combat experiences as an example.

That evening, we were invited to the National Jewish War Veteran Convention banquet at the Omni Hotel in Jacksonville, Florida. General Blum was the keynote speaker. He informed me, "I told them to seat you and Rita close

Largest stained glass American flag in the world, Dole Institute of
Politics, July 20, 2003.

Hal with Lt. Gen. H. Steven Blum, chief of the National Guard Bureau, at OCS Graduation, Camp Blanding, August 9, 2003.

Hal and Rita on the dais with General Blum, the keynote speaker at the National Reunion of Jewish War Veterans, August 9, 2003.

to me. I will be embarrassing you again tonight." As it turned out, we were seated next to him on the dais. He made a great talk, despite making me stand up and praising me to these veterans. Had this man been my general, I would have followed him through hell. He is a great leader. General Blum autographed my program folder, "To my hero Hal." However, he is truly *my* hero.

In September, Rita and I took a three-week cruise on the *Golden Princess*. This cruise went through the Mediterranean, Spain, and then France. I was asked to speak to a standing-room-only crowd on September 12. The next day we went on a tour to the Normandy beaches. On our tour from Le Havre, we stopped at the Arromanches D-Day Museum. The director and his staff recognized me from their books and asked me to sign their special guest book. I autographed books written by Laurent Lefebvre, a French friend, author of *They Were on Utah Beach: 71 Eyewitnesses.* After lunch, the guide on our bus allowed me to talk about Omaha Beach to my fellow travelers. When we arrived at the American cemetery at Colville, our French friends Margaret and Jean Heesen were waiting for us, holding a U.S. flag and a copy of my book. There were embraces, kisses, tears, and Rita was given a box of cookies.

Due to the tight scheduling, I had to rush to visit my buddies' graves. After visits to Lt. Harold Donaldson's and Bedford Hoback's graves, I had to run across the cemetery's mall in order to have time to see a third soldier's resting place. There were two yellow ropes bordering the confines of the mall. I navigated over the first one, but the second one trapped my left foot. I became airborne, my sunglasses flew off, and I hit a sidewalk edge with my nose and forehead. As two French people helped me up, I was bleeding profusely from a wound at the base of my nose. My shirt and blue jacket were drenched with blood. Pressing a handkerchief over the wound, I proceeded to visit Nicholas Kafkalas' grave. Then I rushed to catch our tour bus, where Rita almost passed out upon seeing my blood. My French friends said, "Now Hal has his sixth wound in Normandy." I applied two BAND-AIDs to the deep wound, almost between my eyes. Despite my injury, as the bus moved along Omaha Beach, I enjoyed speaking to the passengers over a microphone. I was able to show them Vierville, the Twenty-ninth Division monument, the pillboxes, and the beach. My injury was very mysterious. According to my knowledge of medicine, I should have sustained a fractured nose and a concussion. Seemingly, my deceased buddies, in some eerie way, protected me. My deep wound was never sutured but healed completely scar free in four days. I had no residual medical problems.

For Veterans' Day, November 11, 2003, Rita and I were flown to Atlanta, Georgia. I addressed twelve hundred students, faculty, and parents at the Westminster Schools. After my talk I spent about two hours in a one-on-one question and answer session with the students. These were the people I wanted to reach. This young audience is not taught the history of D-Day in school, and I fear that the stories of heroism and loss may be forgotten by this generation. An Atlanta teenager, Patrick Walker, was responsible for my being invited. He had bought my book and then prevailed on the school to invite me to speak on Veterans' Day.

December 4, 2003, Rita and I were flown to New Orleans, Louisiana, by the National World War II Museum. We were housed in the Concierge Tower of the Ritz-Carlton Hotel. That afternoon I autographed about fifty of my books as surprise Christmas gifts for each member of the museum's board of trustees. The members of the board of trustees are great people. Through their efforts and generosity, they insure that the D-Day story will never be forgotten. That evening, we attended a banquet in the Louisiana Memorial Pavilion of the museum. I was the keynote speaker, giving the audience an eyewitness account of Dog Green sector on D-Day.

Back in September, the National World War II Museum had arranged for me to be interviewed by Gary Wray, in Ocean City, Maryland, for a DVD commemorating the sixtieth anniversary of D-Day. This was done while I was attending a Twenty-ninth Division annual reunion. The recording is sold by the bookstore of the National World War II Museum as a three DVD pack labeled *D-Day.*

The evening following my keynote speech, we were guests at a dinner party in the French Quarter home of Corrine "Lindy" Boggs. Mrs. Boggs, the mother of Cokie Roberts, the television and National Public Radio news personality,

Hal being introduced just prior to giving a speech to twelve hundred students and faculty at Westminster Private School, Atlanta, Georgia, November 11, 2003.

Hal Baumgarten with French teacher and students of Westminster Private School, Atlanta, Georgia, November 11, 2003.

was the first woman in Congress from Louisiana and has served as the ambassador to the Vatican. Outside her home were revelers and drunks; however, once we entered her green door, we were in a palace. We had cocktails in a court-yard with a fountain and gas heaters to keep us warm. The dinner was a catered, super-gourmet one. Lindy's home was magnificent; even the bathroom had a crystal chandelier. She is a gracious, beautiful hostess, who made us feel welcome. It was a beautiful way to end my year and a welcome break between my 2003 talks and the wealth of engagements facing me in the coming year.

XXIII

The Sixtieth Anniversary of D-Day

A MEDIA BLITZ

The year 2004 was a media blitz. I had thought that the media bonanza of the fiftieth anniversary of D-Day would never be surpassed. At that time, I had been written up in *People* magazine, *USA Today*, and *U.S. News and World Report*. Frank Sessno of CNN and Bob Edwards of NPR had interviewed me. Charles Durning had presented my story dramatically on National Public Television in front of the Capitol. However, all this unsolicited publicity was dwarfed by the tremendous media demand of the sixtieth anniversary of D-Day. It seems that every week I was interviewed, videotaped, and written up in newspapers and magazines such as *Time*. I was flown to various places in the U.S. and Europe for television interviews viewed in the United States, Austria, France, and Germany. The German program was also shown later on the History Channel. In January, while I was attending the annual reunion of the Florida West Post #2 of the Twenty-ninth Division Association in Punta Gorda, Florida, Raimund Loew interviewed me for a segment to be aired on Austrian television. Directly after the interview, Mr.

Loew's cameraman videotaped Rita and I strolling along the shore of the Peace River. The film was excellent.

March 2004 was a busy month for me, as my family celebrated a humongous wedding weekend. Our son, Hal, married Brenda Portnoy on March 20. On March 30, the University of Miami flew me down to Coral Gables, Florida, to speak about D-Day. I was to be the 2004 Estelle and Emil Gould Humanities Lecturer, hosted by the College of Arts and Sciences and the History Department. This lecture series was established in 1977 by Estell and Emil's daughter, Taffy Gould, a celebrity in her own right, in order to honor her parents. When I looked at the list of the previous lecturers, I felt tremendously humbled and honored. People like Winston Churchill's granddaughter and actor Michael York had also lectured for this series. Ms. Gould was a delightful and very interesting young lady. The lecture organizers housed me in the luxurious Biltmore Hotel in Coral Gables, Florida. Upon entering this hotel on the morning of March 30, I immediately felt a sense of déjà vu. The building in which the hotel was located had previously served as the Veterans' Administration Hospital where I had had foot surgery during the summer of 1955.

Associate Dean Paul B. Mischler was my companion for a tour of the University of Miami's huge, beautiful campus. I was feted at a gourmet luncheon, in the office of Dr. James H. Wyche, vice provost and dean of the College of Arts and Sciences. We did not eat this well when I was on the faculty in 1948. Dr. Wyche said that the fine meal was in my honor. Present at lunch were Jane Connolly, senior associate dean of Arts and Humanities; Paul B. Mischler, associate dean for Development and College Relations; Guido Ruggiero, chairman of the Department of History; Edward Dreyer, professor of history and a famous author; and John Gustavsen, graduate student in history. The latter two had a specific interest in military history. We had a lively and interesting discussion during lunch.

At 5:00 P.M., I was escorted to the Judaic Studies Auditorium of the Merrick Building for my talk. I remembered, as a student, seeing the Merrick Building being erected. After very flattering introductions by Dean Wyche and Dr. Ruggiero, I began to talk to about three hundred history buffs and veterans. Unbeknownst to me, Tom Brokaw had an NBC camera crew there to film me. In retrospect, he was probably screen testing me for his NBC sixtieth anniversary of D-Day program. At the start of my talk, I stopped to introduce my good friend and the trustee of the National World War II Museum, John Kushner. He had been instrumental in the University of Miami's inviting me. After speaking for about ten minutes, I spotted my daughter Karen in the audience. I was so surprised that I lost my train of thought momentarily. Karen had flown from New Orleans with Mr. Kushner in order to surprise me. This, she definitely did. I had Karen stand up and introduced her to the audience. She is a practicing attorney and a marathon runner. After my talk, the question and answer session became so prolonged that Dr. Mischler had to put a halt to it. He presented me with an inscribed glass book in a jewelry box to mark the occasion. It had the following inscription:

College of Arts and Sciences
University of Miami
Harold Baumgarten, MS '49, MD '60
With Appreciation
March 30, 2004

A patio reception with great food and drink followed the lecture; however, between embracing my daughter, answering more queries, and fielding the television cameras, I couldn't enjoy it. Though the reception was chaotic, I did have the thrill of meeting Donna E. Shalala, president of the university and a former member of President Clinton's cabinet. She and selected guests honored me later that evening with a dinner at the Deering Bay Yacht and Country Club. She made an eloquent talk, which she ended by looking down at me and saying, "Welcome home." Then she lifted her glass of water and made a toast, saying, "A proper toast for our honored guest is *L'Chaim*." It was a tremendous honor for me to return to my alma mater in this fashion. The next morning, while waiting for my ride to the airport, I walked around the grounds of the Biltmore. My University of Miami medical school, which was on the side of the building, was now the garage of the Biltmore.

April 2004 was a blockbuster month of interviews. I was flown to Los Angeles, California, housed in the Sportsman Lodge, and interviewed at Universal Studios for the filming of "Mail Call," which airs on the History Channel. I was very honored to be selected for this masterpiece of a program about D-Day. Mainly featuring former Ranger "superhero" Len Lomell and myself, it aired on the History Channel as "Mail Call: D-Day Special." This is one of the best pieces of historic coverage about D-Day.

Also in April, producer Ben Burnstein of CNN interviewed me at my condo in Florida. The title of the program was "A Call to Courage," hosted by Paula Zahn. CNN aired "A Call to Courage" on June 6, and all day on July 4, 2004. It featured Len Lomell, Dick Winters, of *Band of Brothers* fame, Marvin Perrett, a brave coast guard veteran, and me. The program had commentators such as Martin Morgan, a research historian at the National World War II Museum, Walter Cronkite, the "dean" of TV anchormen, and John Eisenhower, son of the former president. Ben Burnstein did a terrific job editing the program, and we became good friends.

Hal with Donna Shalala, president of the University of Miami, at the patio reception following his Gould Humanitarian Lecture, March 30, 2004.

On April 29, NBC flew me first class to New Orleans, Louisiana. I was housed in the luxurious Loews New Orleans Hotel. The next morning, Eric Wishnie, Tom Brokaw's senior producer, interviewed me in the National World War II Museum. An outstanding part of the interview included me holding my D-Day wrist watch, which is regularly on display at the museum. I showed Eric, while being filmed, that the watch was still functioning. The next morning, the entire crew was at my condo in Jacksonville Beach, Florida. This filming lasted about six hours, culminating with Rita and I walking and talking on the beach. Meaghan Rady, associate producer, made all the hotel and transportation arrangements for me. She is an angel. In June, NBC completed the film with part three in France.

May was another very busy month. *Time Magazine* interviewed me on May 1 for their May 31, 2004, issue. They sent a photographer to Jacksonville Beach, Florida, who took one hundred photos, but only used one of them, a photo of me on the beach. On May 9 and 10, I had a French television crew at my condo. They didn't converse well in English, so I had to find an interpreter, Renee Lescott, who did a great job of interpreting for two days. The crew filmed footage for a one-hour program called "Sept à Huit," which was seen by seven million French people. I recently received a copy of the film, and except for the lighting, it was very good. Three days after the departure of the French film crew, WJCT-TV Miami interviewed me on *New Florida,* a weekly television magazine. Joyce Beloise was the producer of this excellent program, which aired on May 28. That month, I was also interviewed on local television channel 4 and by the local affiliates of CBS, ABC, and NBC television networks. Unfortunately, I had to turn down interviews with Wolf Blitzer, CNN, and Diane Sawyer due to the utter lack of time; however John Grady of the U.S. Army News and the

Italian newspaper *La Stampa* did have the opportunity to interview me.

On May 27, Lt. David Coffman, of the Jacksonville Police Department, picked up Rita and I for the Sheriff's Monthly Awards Ceremony. I was called to come up to the front of their auditorium and presented with two plaques. Sheriff Rutherford presented one of the plaques, which said, "In appreciation for meritorious service to the citizens of Jacksonville." Lieutenant Coffman of the Police Mobile Field Forces presented the second beautiful wooden plaque. It was presented "for reminding us that leadership, training, and discipline are critical in our daily survival." This was a very proud moment for me. I received a standing ovation from the police and guests. The awards were given in thanks for the three occasions that I had spoken at the police academy.

On June 4, Rita and I were scheduled to be flown to London by the National World War II Museum, for I was going to be a lecturer on their sixtieth anniversary tour. We were to board the luxurious *Silver Cloud* cruise ship in London Harbor on June 4 and cruise to Caen, Normandy; however, we discovered that Tom Brokaw had other plans for us. Instead, he sent us first class to Paris on June 1 in order to complete part three of NBC's sixtieth anniversary film. I was in danger of getting spoiled with limousines transporting me and first-class flights across the Atlantic Ocean. When we boarded the Air France flight headed for Paris, a male steward said, "I know you." He had seen me on French television. As we approached the French coast, the captain invited me to join him in the cockpit. He pointed out Omaha Beach, Cherbourg, and Saint-Lô to me. He autographed and gave me the plane's navigation map: "AF Flight #29, June 2, 2004—Dear Harold: Your grateful Captain Pat Bourgouin and his crew."

When we arrived in Paris, we were picked up by a limo

and transported to our hotel, adjacent to the Champs-Élysée, where we were housed in a magnificent suite. Since Rita did not care to fly in a helicopter to Normandy, she was left in Paris to "suffer," providing her plenty of time to sightsee and shop. It was approaching our fifty-fifth wedding anniversary. I left early in the morning on June 3 in order to catch the awaiting helicopter. The flight over the beautiful city of Paris was thrilling. I could see the Place Charles De Gaulle-Etoile (Arc de Triomphe de l'Etoile), the Eiffel Tower, and la Basilique du Sacré-Coeur. We arrived at Charles De Gaulle Airport and were soon joined by Tom and Meredith Brokaw. Tom introduced me to the beautiful Meredith as the veteran that spoke at the opening of the National World War II Museum. She responded that she remembered me. Then Tom looked at me and gave me the greatest compliment I ever received in my life. He said, "After you spoke, I didn't want to get up to speak." I only wish I had his good looks, poise, and wonderful, booming voice.

The three of us flew to a chateau in Bayeux, Normandy. We landed on the front lawn of this majestic chateau, and Eric Wishnie joined us. Refreshments were served in a glass-enclosed sunroom. After freshening up, Tom, Eric, and I, accompanied by a photographer, took off in the whirlybird for Omaha Beach. Tom requested that we fly very low over Omaha Beach, then he started broadcasting, with no script. We finally landed at an army base and took a limousine to the Dog Green sector of Omaha Beach. They had warned me to wear old shoes. Tom and I were wired for sound and walked out to the water's edge. I told him that he could ask me any questions, and I would give him a good response. There was no rehearsal or script. In fact, in all my mentioned interviews, there were never any scripts.

Thus, Tom and I walked on the hallowed sands of the Dog Green beach while conversing and being filmed.

Afterward we retreated to NBC's cemetery headquarters tent, where there were dozens of people working on the sixtieth anniversary reporting. Tom sat down at his computer and started working. After some refreshments, Eric (my genius friend) wanted to do the final "shoot" in the American cemetery. Tom got up from his computer and gave me a goodbye hug. He handed me one of his books. I said, "Tom, I have your book." He replied, "You don't have this book." I cannot say enough about what a great person Tom Brokaw is. After I had completed the filming of my segments and while I was in the helicopter returning to Paris, I looked at the book he had presented me. It was autographed, "To Hal: One of the greatest of the greatest—Tom Brokaw." Needless to say, when I returned home, I replaced my old copy with this valuable personalized new copy.

Having said my good-byes to Tom Brokaw, I met sweet

If not for God, this would have been Hal's grave

Hal at 1st Lt. Harold Donaldson's grave at the American
cemetery, Colville, Normandy.

Meaghan Rady for the first time in person. She drove the
golf cart with Eric, a photographer, and me. When I alight-
ed from the cart, I happened to be standing at Elmere P.
Wright's grave (Company A, 116th). I had crawled past his
lifeless body at about 7:00 A.M. on D-Day. The producers
wanted to film me approaching and then standing at Lt.
Harold Donaldson's grave. I purposely started walking from
a Star of David, because German television had not show
any of those markers in their own D-Day programming. As
is a Jewish tradition, I placed a small black stone, with
Harold's name on it, on his cross, stepped back, and saluted. All this was captured on film and used. I had brought
three black marble stones, all with my buddies' names

engraved on them. My lovely friends Elizabeth and Nicholas Barranca of Ijamsville, Maryland, provided these stones.

Eric Wishnie took the three interviews, and with his artistic genius, he was able to produce a wonderful seven-minute NBC *Nightly News* masterpiece program. It played on NBC on June 5, but I did not see it; however, I spoke to Steven Spielberg and Tom Hanks on June 6 in the Colville American cemetery, and they raved about the Brokaw program. Tom Brokaw had given them a private showing. Mr. Spielberg told me the same thing that my good friend Dr. Ambrose once said to me: "Your story is most amazing." Tom Brokaw used this film on his final NBC *Nightly News* program, and Eric Wishnie is still my good friend.

When I arrived back in Paris that evening, Rita and I had to go to Charles De Gaulle airport for a British Airways flight to London. That evening we slept in London. On June 4, we boarded the *Silver Cloud,* a six-star luxury cruise ship, for the sixtieth anniversary tour of the National World War II Museum. We had a great cadre of speakers on the tour, and about 250 very interested history buffs eager to hear about D-Day. The speakers, besides myself, were Gerald Astor, Donald Miller, Ronald Drez, and Viscount David Montgomery, all well-known historians. Another veteran on our trip was Walter Ehlers, a Congressional Medal of Honor winner. The people on this trip were a marvelous group. Besides the D-Day Museum officials like Dr. Gordon Mueller, CEO, Hugh Ambrose, vice-president, and Peter McLean, Yakir Katz, and Bosie Bollinger and their charming wives, there was also John Kushner, a trustee, who calls himself my number-one fan—he and his vivacious wife, Barbara. It was a great pleasure having the opportunity to speak to these folks, who were all interested in D-Day and the preservation of the World War II Museum. My special friends on the board of trustees, other than the ones mentioned above, were Allan Franco and Frank Stewart and their lovely wives.

On June 5, the ship cruised off the coast of Omaha Beach, and I spoke on the deck. What a thrill for me to view Dog Green sector and the Vierville church steeple from the English Channel for the first time in sixty years. Subsequently, I was able to talk to the people from our ship on a tour bus that took us to the beaches and Pointe du Hoc. We even visited the Forbes family chateau one day and had champagne and hors d'oeuvres. We later traveled up the Seine River, visiting Bruges, Belgium, Monet's beautiful home in Giverny, and ended up in Amsterdam, Netherlands. Throughout this trip, I was autographing my article in *Time Magazine*. I had never realized that *Time* was sold in Europe.

One day, a very nice couple we knew only as Pete and Gayle asked Rita and I to join them for lunch and dinner. They were from California and looked like movie stars. At dinner, Pete refused to drink the complementary French wine. He only wanted California wine. In the course of conversation, Rita inquired about his occupation. He replied, "Oh, I am the former governor of California" (Pete Wilson). We enjoyed their company. Unfortunately, they had to leave the cruise abruptly when President Reagan died. They had to attend the funeral.

For July 4, I was interviewed by a dynamic radio personality, Jordan Rich, of WBZ Radio in Boston, Massachusetts. His program is heard in thirty-eight states as well as in Canada. Alexander Kershaw, a famous author and screenwriter and a good friend of mine, had been interviewed the night before. He spoke very flatteringly about me. Also in July, I was interviewed at my condo and on the beach nearby for a documentary called *Overlord—A Mighty Host*. It was produced by Brad Stokes of ABC Family and it aired on that network.

Just when I thought all such honors were over—it does get embarrassing—I was awarded a plaque by the Twenty-ninth Division Association at the annual reunion held at Tyson Corners, Virginia, on October 9. I almost didn't show up for this meeting because I was invited to speak at the annual air force formal banquet in Belgium, hosted by the European Supreme Air Command. They were going to fly Rita and I to Belgium, but I turned them down rather than miss my Twenty-niner meeting. It's a good thing I did. This surprise award was made at our banquet in the presence of the governor of Maryland, Bob Ehrlich, and Maj. Gen. Wyman, commanding officer of the Twenty-ninth Division Light. Retired major general Boyd Cook, my good friend and the former commanding officer of the Twenty-ninth Division Light, made the presentation. He mentioned that I had given up speaking in Belgium that very evening, but I felt that to receive an award from my Twenty-ninth Division buddies was more important and tear provoking than any other accolade. The plaque states:

> *Our Association proudly salutes*
> *Harold Baumgarten, MD*
> *D-Day B Company 116th Infantry*
> *29th Division*
> *"Our Ambassador of Goodwill"*
> *For his 62 years of Service to*
> *Our Country and to Our Association*
> *9 October 2004*

Not long after such a touching tribute from my comrades, the class of 1954 of Palm Beach High School invited me to be their keynote speaker at their fiftieth anniversary banquet in West Palm Beach, Florida, on October 30. Though I had been their teacher and had been very active in their school lives, they were not aware of my D-Day experiences, so I

Hal receiving award as "Ambassador of Goodwill" from the Twenty-ninth Division Association. Presented by Gen. Boyd Cook at annual reunion, October 9, 2004.

talked about my life before coming to their school in 1951. These alumni, who were within a decade of my age, were not only shocked, but mesmerized by my talk. A few had remembered asking me about the scar on my left cheek and being advised that it was an "old scratch." This evening was very memorable for me because as I gazed at these people, I realized that God had spared me on D-Day for another reason. They were now aeronautical engineers, lawyers, physicians, college professors, and good citizens, and I had played a small part in influencing their lives.

At this West Palm Beach, Florida event, I received a phone call from Stephen McPherson, president of ABC Entertainment. He told me that ABC Television was going to present the film *Saving Private Ryan* on national TV for Veterans' Day, November 11, 2004. He stated that Steven Spielberg wanted him to show the movie "uncut," and that he had requested that I host the program. This was unbelievable to me. Had he not mentioned Mr. Spielberg's name, I would have turned him down, as Rita and I were all packed to go on a very long trip to Thailand.

Thus on November 4, I was flown first class to Honolulu, Oahu, placed in the luxurious Princess Hotel, and wined and dined. Rita was invited, but opted not to go. She was preparing herself for the very long flight to Thailand. The ABC crew was very nice to me. On November 5, we shot the program introduction at Pearl Harbor. Newly elected senator John McCain of Arizona, a fine man and a great American, was my co-host. I was to welcome the viewers and introduce the film, and John was going to give the viewer disclaimer. While waiting to film, I was presented with a captain's cap from the battleship docked beside us. This was the famous battleship *Missouri*, where the Japanese surrender had taken place. This gift was from the U.S. Navy League, of which I am a member.

It was raining during the shoot, but the program came

out perfectly. The ABC producers and the lighting, sound, and makeup people were excellent. Margaret Conley and Andrea Taylor, producers of the ABC series *Lost*, watched out for me. We and the other crewmembers, Dan Staedler and Lee Redmond, had a few great dinners together. The last evening, we celebrated; I had two Johnnie Walker Black scotches. We toasted a very successful shoot under very trying weather conditions.

It was incredible that some cities banned the showing of the movie because of its uncut, adult content and language. In Florida, Tampa and Orlando banned the showing of this epic film. I gave an interview on local TV advising why it should not be banned. On November 12, I received a personal thank-you letter from Mr. Spielberg, who was very

Sen. John McCain and Hal hosting *Saving Private Ryan* special at Pearl Harbor, November 2004.

Left around to right: Len Richmond, Dan Staedler, Andrea Taylor, and Margaret Conley of ABC crew, with Hal Baumgarten.

upset by the widespread banning of this viewing of *Saving Private Ryan.* I also received a bottle of Johnnie Walker Blue scotch and a thank-you letter from Mr. McPherson. His letter stated, "Spielberg was right about you. I understand you indulge in a scotch, once in a while, so enjoy."

The media blitz in 2004 did more to keep the D-Day story alive than at any previous year. My story and those of my buddies were recorded on U.S., French, German, and Austrian television. I feel certain that after these programs and a write-up in *Time Magazine,* I have fulfilled my promise to my buddies that they never be forgotten.

Chapter XXIV

Family

MY LEGACY

This book cannot be completed without some information about my family. I have already related about meeting my wife Rita in 1948, and how she has been the love of my life for the past fifty-six years. However, I haven't mentioned much about my children and grandchildren.

Our first child, Karen Rae, was born in West Palm Beach, Florida, on December 26, 1952. I was teaching at Palm Beach High School at that time and had ample time to be a good father. We took her for rides every afternoon, except during football season, because I was also a coach. I remember that she had a sweet tooth and enjoyed her Dairy Queen chocolate-dipped cones. In the summer we took her to the Sun and Surf Club in Palm Beach to play on the beach and swim. We were also able to take her on frequent visits to her maternal grandparents in Miami Beach, where we enjoyed swimming and attending shows. We would also send her to visit her paternal grandparents in River Edge, New Jersey.

During my stint in medical school, I neglected my fatherly duties most of the year; however, Karen had a loving mother very capable of taking up the parenting slack, and our neighborhood always had many friends of Karen's age, so she never lacked playmates. During my summer breaks from medical school, I was able to take Karen, along with her new sister, Bonnie, on vacations. We went to Gatlinburg and Ruby Falls, Tennessee, New York, and to all the Florida tourist attractions.

Karen was an excellent student in the public schools of Miami, and later, Jacksonville, Florida. When she graduated from Wolfson High School, she won the Spanish award. Karen was accepted, early decision, to the elite Sophie Newcomb College of Tulane University, in New Orleans, Louisiana. This prestigious school is sometimes referred to as the "Vassar of the South." She graduated with honors and was listed in *Who's Who Among Students*.

Since Karen always was a great debater with us at home, she was a natural to become a lawyer. Thus, Karen started attending Tulane Law School. On June 7, 1975, she married one of her fellow law students, Leopold Sher. Lee graduated one year ahead of Karen and now has his own law firm in New Orleans. After her own graduation, Karen worked for the Fifth District Circuit Court of Appeals until she took leave to raise their two daughters. Incidentally, Karen has returned to practicing law in New Orleans.

In addition to being a super mom, she is an athlete. While in college, she was on the women's water ballet team; however, in recent years she has become a regular jogger and has run in the New Orleans, Boston, and Chicago marathons.

My son-in-law Leopold comes from a very religious family. His parents and relatives had suffered the cruelty, starvation, and indignities of Nazi concentration camps. Lee and his brother, Martin, were brought up in a very Orthodox Jewish atmosphere, their parents, Joseph and Rachael Sher, keeping a kosher home. As a result of their influence, Karen became very religious and also established a kosher home. Unfortunately, sweet Rachael has passed away; however, Joe is still going strong. He lectures about the Holocaust in order to keep the horrible history alive.

Karen and Leopold have always made me proud of them. They are both outstanding people. This love match of thirty years produced two wonderful granddaughters. Rose Sarah was the first born, and my second-oldest grandchild. She attended and graduated with honors from Isidore Newman School in New Orleans. Rose is twenty-two and graduated from the University of Southern California's Annenberg School of Journalism with honors on May 12, 2006.

Samantha Jill, Rose's sister, is eighteen years old and a former honor student at Newman. Sam was elected vice president of her senior class and was recognized on the football field for the school's homecoming court. Modeling has been one of her afterschool activities. In addition, she was on the cross-country and track teams, running relays and even pole-vaulting. On applying for early decision admission to attend the University of Pennsylvania, she was immediately accepted and in 2006 had successfully completed her freshman year at that university.

Any grandfather would be proud of girls like these. My granddaughters are not only gorgeous on the outside, but also good, religious individuals, very intelligent and sweet. There is no doubt my granddaughters inherited their beauty from their mother. Both of my daughters are attractive enough to be movie stars, no doubt due to my wife's good looks.

Bonnie Sue, my second child, was born at Jackson Memorial Hospital in Miami, Florida, during my sophomore year of medical school. She is very precious to me. Bonnie was my "neglected" child, due to my studying around the clock. Despite this, my relationship with Bonnie has always been great. No matter what I say to her, she never argues, and she never gets angry with me. She has always been extremely affectionate.

Bonnie was an excellent student in the public schools of Jacksonville, where her interests were in the field of science. She skipped from her junior year at Wolfson High School straight into Jacksonville University. Though Bonnie attended college in her hometown, residing in the dormitory made her feel like she was living away from home. However, after one year, she transferred to Florida State University in Tallahassee. After she received her B.S. degree and did some teaching, she matriculated at the University of Houston. Bonnie graduated from the University of Houston with a master of education degree and became the youngest member of their faculty, with health education as her focal subject.

Bonnie was married to a gynecologist in Houston. This union, while it did not last long, gave me my first grandchild, Michael Louis. He was the most beautiful child I had ever seen. Bonnie and her husband divorced, but her next marriage was to Ken Friedman. This lasting marriage produced twin grandchildren, Katy Rose and Matthew David. Bonnie's marriage to Ken has been loving and very successful. Ken is an excellent businessman whose office places executives with various large corporations. Bonnie, who, as the mother of young twins, was unhappy with teaching, decided to become a travel agent. She became so successful that she opened her own agency, VIP Vacations, Inc., in Longwood, Florida. I am one of her travel clients.

My oldest grandchild, Michael, is twenty-two years old and attends the University of South Florida, near Tampa. He has a tremendous talent for music, which he probably inherited from his father. Rita and I attended his high school football games, and watched him perform in the marching band. Today he is a founding member of his own jazz band. Katy and Matthew are seventeen years old. They both have beautiful velvet blue eyes and are outstandingly good looking, as all my grandchildren seem to be. Katy, very sweet as well as lovely, is the "artsy" one, making wallets and knitting scarves.

Matthew is the "academic" one, with a straight A average. He wants to become a lawyer like his aunt Karen.

Hal, my last child and only son, was born at Baptist Medical Center in Jacksonville, Florida, on May 23, 1965. He was always a good child, but he became distracted when he found out about girls; as a result, his schoolwork suffered. After he graduated from Wolfson High School, he attended Mercer University in Macon, Georgia, where he made the dean's list and graduated with a bachelor's degree with a double major in psychology and sociology. He took his postgraduate studies at the University of Texas at Austin, spent a semester at the University of Florida in Gainesville, and was accepted to graduate school at Norwich University of Montpellier, Vermont, in order to pursue a master's degree in counseling psychology. Unfortunately, due to divorce he was unable to complete his graduate-level studies.

Hal eventually became interested in the financial services industry. During his employment with Bank of America, he received many awards and became the top consumer banker in the state of Florida, wherein he was awarded an all-expenses paid trip to Maui. Hal recently began working as a senior financial services specialist and continues to pursue his career goals in the financial industry. Outside of work, Hal is a very talented pianist and writes his own music. He and his friends had their own band in high school. It is too bad that he never tried to publish any of his music.

His first marriage gave me a sweet granddaughter, Rachel Sarah. Rachel is now fifteen years old. She inherited her father's musical talent and can play the piano beautifully as well as the harmonica. Today, Hal is married happily to Brenda Portnoy, a graduate of the University of North Florida. She is intelligent, cute, and has a great personality.

Hal is the only one of my children who shows an interest in D-Day, although Karen is a member of the National World War II Museum. Hal is an associate member of the

Left to right: Hal, Bonnie, and Karen, February 2005.

Twenty-ninth Division Association. He calls Rita and I every day just to say, "I love you."

I am very proud of my children and grandchildren, and love them with all my heart. My children have grown up to be outstandingly good members of society. They do not smoke, drink, or use drugs. They learned a love of good old music and a strong belief in God in our household. My hope for my grandchildren is that they inherit my patriotic fervor. They should love our country the way I do: "My country right or wrong." I have a fear that the liberal "professorial intelligencia" of our present-day colleges, placing one-sided, activist beliefs in today's youth, will negatively influence their fertile, growing minds. Hopefully, our future generations will be observant, focused, and courageous enough to oppose biased onslaughts and seek both sides of the subject matter. It is my desire that my grandchildren become good U.S. citizens and that they never forget their grandfather and D-Day.

Companies A and B, Twenty-ninth Infantry, 116th Regiment

MOVING EVER FORWARD

The Twenty-ninth Infantry Division
"Twenty-nine, Let's Go"

The Twenty-ninth Infantry Division of the U.S. Army can trace its roots back to the militias that fought in the French and Indian Wars. Later elements took part in the Revolutionary War. They fought under distinguished leaders such as Patrick Henry and George Washington. They also fought in the War of 1812 and the Civil War. During the Civil War, some of these militias opposed each other, as Northerners against Southerners. At the beginning of World War I, the modern Twenty-ninth Division was established. The Northerners and the Southerners were now joined into one unit, despite their historic differences.

In recognition of this past disparity, the division's insignia is a symbol of conjunction. It contains both the blue of the North and the gray of the South, side-by-side, on the shoulder patch. The patch was worn on the left shoulder by Twenty-niners in the Meuse-Argonne Offensive of World

War I. In World War II, the blue and gray insignia was worn on the helmets as well as on the shoulder. The Blue and Gray Division, as they were called, fought from Omaha Beach, Normandy, on June 6, 1944, to Bremen, Germany, in May 1945. During this span of time, more than 20,300 men became casualties, likely the most casualties suffered by any U.S. Army division fighting only in the Western European Campaign. It was said of the Twenty-ninth that it was like three outfits: one in the cemetery, one in the hospital, and the other on the fighting line.

The Twenty-ninth Division was always a proud National Guard outfit. For present-day conflicts, it is on active duty and known as the Twenty-ninth Division Light. Former members of the Twenty-ninth Division and their families have bonded together to form the Twenty-ninth Division Association. We have one of the finest quarterly journals, known as the *Twenty-Niner*. Our association and divisional motto, "Twenty-nine, Let's Go," is the battle cry that rallied us off the beach on D-Day. We hold a national reunion each year, usually in the fall. At these meetings, we always honor our members who have answered the final roll call for the year. There are no officers recognized officially in our organization, though I am proud to have been elected national surgeon and to hold the title of "Ambassador of Goodwill." We are one large family of former Twenty-niners and present-day active Twenty-ninth Light men.

The commanding general of the Twenty-ninth on D-Day was Maj. Gen. Charles H. Gerhardt. General Gerhardt, or "Uncle Charlie," as he was called, was a great officer and strict disciplinarian. He was the quarterback of his West Point football team. Brig. Gen. Norman D. Cota was the assistant divisional commander on D-Day. I can attest for both of these men, "They don't come any braver." In recognition of the numerous men of the Twenty-ninth who displayed bravery like that of Generals Gerhardt and Cota, the Twenty-ninth Infantry Division was awarded the Croix de Guerre with Silver Palm for the landing on Omaha and extending the beachhead in June 1944. The Twenty-ninth Division Association opening prayer expresses the merits of this great organization:

> Almighty God, we thank you for the blessings and the freedom you have given us in this great nation. We thank you for the camaraderie that brings us together here today. As we assemble to perpetuate the friendships we cherish, grant that we may always keep alive the spirit that never knew defeat, glorify our dead and ever keep before our country, the record of the Twenty-ninth Division in the World Wars, bless and protect the members of the Twenty-ninth Division Light, in their service. Guide us with your wisdom and love in all our deliberations, and let us not forget our comrades who answered the last roll call. Amen.

I am so proud to have been a part of this great outfit. In combat, any one of these men would lay down his life to save a buddy.

The 116th Infantry Regiment
"Ever Forward"

The 116th Infantry Regiment has a long and noble history with roots in the Second Virginia Regiment from about 1740. Col. George Washington, and later, Col. Patrick Henry, commanded this outfit (1760-75). This same regiment was instrumental in defeating the British in Virginia during the Revolutionary War. Later, during the Civil War, the Second Virginia Regiment fought for the Confederacy. It was part of the famous "Stonewall Brigade," under the command of Gen. Thomas Jonathan "Stonewall" Jackson, for which it was named. This outfit was trained, like my D-Day outfit, to be mobile and hit the enemy hard and rapid. One of its great battles was at Winchester, Virginia, where they captured about eight hundred Union soldiers.

The 116th Infantry distinguished itself in World War I in the Meuse-Argonne fighting. They earned the regiment's motto, "Ever Forward," for never relinquishing a yard in combat. In World War II, the Stonewall Brigade was the spearhead (first wave) of the Twenty-ninth Division's landing on Omaha Beach on D-Day. The commanding officer of the 116th Infantry on D-Day was Col. Charles D. W. Canham. Lt. Col. John A. Metcalfe was the commander of the First Battalion, my outfit. On D-Day, the regiment had 608 casualties, including 341 killed in action and 26 missing in action. The next day there were 189 casualties. Incidentally, the Stonewall Brigade is represented today, with headquarters located in Staunton, Virginia.

The 116th Infantry received a Distinguished Presidential Citation for D-Day. It reads as follows:

> For extraordinary heroism and outstanding performance of duty in action in the initial assault on the northern coast of Normandy, France. On 6 June 1944, the 116th Infantry successfully attacked a heavily defended beach in the vicinity of Vierville-sur-Mer, France. The beach was fortified by mined underwater obstacles, bands of barbed wire, concrete walls, and landmines. It was strongly defended by enemy troops occupying pillboxes, trenches, and underground shelters. Defending troops were protected against aerial and Naval bombardment, which preceded the assault, by deep and elaborate underground shelters, which had been constructed in the hills and cliffs overlooking the beach. In addition, the beach was subjected to fire from enemy artillery and mortars, which were inshore. In the face of this heavy fire and in spite of suffering high losses, the 116th Infantry overcame the beach obstacles, took the enemy-defended positions along the beach and cliffs, pushed through the mined area immediately in rear of the beach while still under heavy fire, and continued inshore to take its objective. The successful assault and landing of the 116th

Infantry made possible subsequent landings of other elements of the Twenty-ninth Division, which landed behind it with only light losses. During its landing and assault of the beach positions, the 116th Infantry sustained more than 800 losses in officers and men.

Companies A and B
"Never Quit Fighting"

Company A of the 116th Infantry was formed from a nucleus of young National Guardsmen from Bedford, Virginia. The original men in Company B of the 116th Infantry were from the Lynchburg, Virginia, area. On D-Day, the commanding officer of Company A was Capt. Taylor N. Fellers. Capt. Ettore V. Zappacosta commanded Company B. By 7:00 A.M., both Companies A and B had landed on the Dog Green sector of Omaha Beach. The commanders of both companies were killed immediately. By 8:00 A.M., I estimate that over 85 percent of the companies' men were casualties. There were no reinforcements sent in to help us fight. As mentioned in this book, we had to continue fighting, despite our wounds. Both companies defeated the enemy that day, but with very heavy losses.

With replacements, Companies A and B never quit fighting. They fought and distinguished themselves in Normandy and through Germany. For the D-Day landing the men of both companies were awarded an arrowhead on their European Theatre of Operations Medals, presidential citations, Combat Infantry Badges, Bronze Star Medals, and lots of Purple Hearts.

I had the honor of being among these great men, and being a part of the Twenty-ninth Division had a great influence on my life. I was placed by providence with a group of fine religious, incredibly patriotic human beings. Since I was spared on D-Day from the horrible deaths suffered by my buddies on the beach, it was incumbent upon me to lead an exemplary life in society for being spared. Fortunately, I have done that through my practice of medicine, teaching, and leading a good, religious life.

Afterword

This book details my amazing life experiences. I realize that I am not immortal and must consider my eventual death. Where am I to be buried? My religion forbids cremation, but it is the service I would prefer, as I doubt my children will visit my synagogue's unimpressive cemetery, which is in a very bad neighborhood. I am eligible to be interred in Arlington National Cemetery, and all the national cemeteries are well kept and respectful to their honorable tenants. This is a decision I have yet to make.

What about my grave marker? In a national cemetery most of the grave markers are simple, standard, small marble markers. Even though I have never considered myself to be a special hero, I would like a marker signifying my life. At President Truman's grave in Independence, Missouri, I noted the slab on his grave listed some of his accomplishments. I would like a slab over my grave, inscribed with "TAPS." This would sum up my life: **T**eacher, **A**uthor, **P**hysician, and **S**oldier.

Acknowledgments

Dr. Stephen E. Ambrose impressed upon me the importance of keeping the D-Day story alive. He prodded me, not only to write about D-Day, but also to speak about it.

Stewart Bryant, who by his relentless pursuit of the history of D-Day, including interviews of German veterans, has proven invaluable to me. He provided information that filled in some blank periods of my D-Day adventure.

Lindsey Reynolds, assistant editor at Pelican Publishing Company, for her fine and patient editing of this book.

And finally, to my son, Hal Baumgarten, for his substantial help in the preparation of this book.

Bibliography

Astor, Gerald. *June 6, 1944: The Voices of D-Day*. New York: St. Martin's Press, 1994.

Ambrose, Stephen E. *D-Day: The Climactic Battle of World War II*. New York: Simon & Schuster, 1994.

———. *The Victors: Eisenhower and His Boys: The Men of World War II*. New York: Simon & Schuster, 1998.

Barnes, John J. *Fragments of My Life with Company A, 116th Infantry*. Holland Patent, N.Y.: JAM Publications, 2000.

Bastable, Jonathan. *Voices from D-Day*. Cincinnati, Ohio: F & W Publications, 2000.

Baumgarten, Harold. *Eyewitness on Omaha Beach*. Jacksonville, Fla.: Halrit Publishing, 1994.

———. *Eyewitness on Omaha Beach: Second Edition*. Jacksonville, Fla.: Halrit Publishing, 2000.

Brinkley, Douglas, and Ronald J. Drez. *Voices of Valor*. New York: Bulfinch Press, 2004.

Cawthon, Charles R. *Other Clay: A Remembrance of the World War II Infantry*. Niwot: University Press of Colorado, 1990.

Drez, Ronald J. *Voices of D-Day*. Baton Rouge: Louisiana State University Press, 1994.

Ewing, Joseph. *29 Let's Go! A History of the 29th Infantry Division in World War II.* Washington, D.C.: Infantry Journal Press, 1948.

Gawne, Jonathan. *Spearheading D-Day.* Paris, France: Histoire & Collections, 1998.

Jensen, Dick. *Normandy Survivors.* Alexander, N.C.: Alexander Books, 2004.

Keeney, Douglas, and William S. Butler. *Day of Destiny.* New York: William Morrow and Company, Inc., 1998.

Kershaw, Alex. *The Bedford Boys: One American Town's Ultimate D-Day Sacrifice.* Cambridge, Mass.: De Capo Press, 2003.

Miller, Russell. *Nothing Less Than Victory: The Oral History of D-Day.* New York: William Morrow and Company, Inc., 1993.

Schildt, John W. *The Long Line of Splendor, 1742-1992.* Chewsville, Md.: Antietam Press, 1993.

War Department. *Omaha Beachhead.* Washington, D.C.: Historical Division, 1945.

Worley, Donald H. *"We Did What We Had to Do": American Stories from World War II.* Chapel Hill, North Carolina: Professional Press, 1995.

Index

The Author

Dr. Harold "Hal" Baumgarten is a multidecorated survivor of the first-wave landing on Dog Green sector of Omaha Beach on D-Day, June 6, 1944. He was silent on his wartime memories until his first trip back to Normandy, France, in 1988. When he looked at the graves of his buddies in the Normandy American Cemetery and Memorial at Colville, he realized that God had spared him to be their spokesman. These true heroes of D-Day must never be forgotten. Thus, he wrote two self-published books on D-Day called *Eyewitness on Omaha Beach,* which is sold in France as *Temoin sur Omaha Beach.* Hal then embarked upon several speaking tours, speaking all over the United States, South America, and Europe about D-Day. His most recent tours have taken him back to Omaha Beach. Hal returned to Normandy as a part of the National World War II Museum's Normandy Tour on June 6, 2006. He laid a wreath at the American cemetery to honor his D-Day buddies and shared stories about these real heroes of D-Day. In September 2006, Hal once again returned to the Dog Green sector as a speaker for the second part of the National World War II Museum's tour.

His exploits have been recorded in the National World War II Museum, *Yank Magazine*, the *New York Daily Mirror*, *People Magazine*, *Time Magazine*, *U.S. News and World Report*, *U.S.A. Today*, the *Richmond Times-Dispatch*, *U.S. Army News*, Italy's *La Stampa*, the *Florida Times-Union*, the *Beaches Leader*, *Mature Matters Magazine*, every Knight-Ridder newspaper, and even the *Encyclopedia Britannica*. Forty books, including his own, published in the U.S. and France, mention Hal's experiences. Bob Edwards dramatized Hal's D-Day activities on NPR's *Morning Edition*. Jordan Rich of WBZ Radio has interviewed him, and many TV programs from the United States, Austria, France, and Germany have featured him. Hal has spoken at schools and libraries and for clubs and civic and professional organizations. He was the Gould Humanities Lecturer in 2004 at the University of Miami. Steven Spielberg even requested that Hal host the showing of his *Saving Private Ryan* on ABC television on Veterans' Day 2004.

After discharge from the service, Hal returned to New York University to receive his bachelor's degree and earned his master's degree from the University of Miami. Realizing that God had spared him in part to become a physician and help his fellow man, he attended the University of Miami School of Medicine, receiving his medical doctorate degree. He is board certified in family medicine and practiced industrial surgery throughout his career. In addition, Hal was the medical director of Gulf Life Insurance Company, a subsidiary of American General Life Insurance Company, until 1992. That year he became a part-time physician with the Veterans' Administration, from which he retired in 1998.

Hal's wife, Rita, has been the light of his life for nearly sixty years, and he has three wonderful children and six precious grandchildren. He resides in beautiful Jacksonville Beach, Florida.